Third Edition

SALES

PROMOTION

ESSENTIALS

Third Edition

DON E. SCHULTZ
WILLIAM A. ROBINSON
LISA A. PETRISON

SALES

PROMOTION

ESSENTIALS

The 10 Basic Sales Promotion Techniques... and How to Use Them

NTC Business Books
NTC/Contemporary Publishing Company

Library of Congress Cataloging-in-Publication Data
is available from the United States Library of Congress.

Interior design by Jeanette Wojtyla

Published by NTC Business Books
An imprint of NTC/Contemporary Publishing Company
4255 West Touhy Avenue, Lincolnwood (Chicago), Illinois 60646-1975 U.S.A.
Copyright © 1998 by NTC/Contemporary Publishing Company
Printed in the United States of America
International Standard Book Number: 0-8442-3354-4 (cloth)
0-8442-3355-2 (paper)
18   17   16   15   14   13   12   11   10   9   8   7   6   5   4   3   2   1

Contents

CHAPTER TWELVE

Price Discounts   187

CHAPTER THIRTEEN

Trade Deals   203

Index   223

CHAPTER ONE

Sales Promotion: Introduction and Current Trends

S ales promotion in the United States is a big, big business—and one that is continuing to grow significantly each year. Consider these facts:

- Sales promotion represents nearly three-fourths of the marketing budget at most consumer-products companies.

- In 1995, trade promotion represented 51 percent of marketers' total promotional budgets, consumer promotion represented 24 percent, and media advertising represented 25 percent. (In 1980, 34 percent of expenditures were on trade promotion, 22 percent were on consumer promotion, and 44 percent were on media advertising.)

- About one-third of consumer-products companies' spending on media advertising is designed to support trade or consumer sales promotions.

- Nearly 300 billion coupons (3,000 for every U.S. household) were distributed in the United States in 1995, up from 40 billion in 1975.

- Consumers saved $4 billion by redeeming about 7 billion coupons in 1995. Almost 90 percent of consumers reported using coupons during the past six months, and nearly 30 percent of all consumers state they use coupons on all shopping trips.

Exhibit 1.1   Share of Promotional Dollars–Long-Term Trend

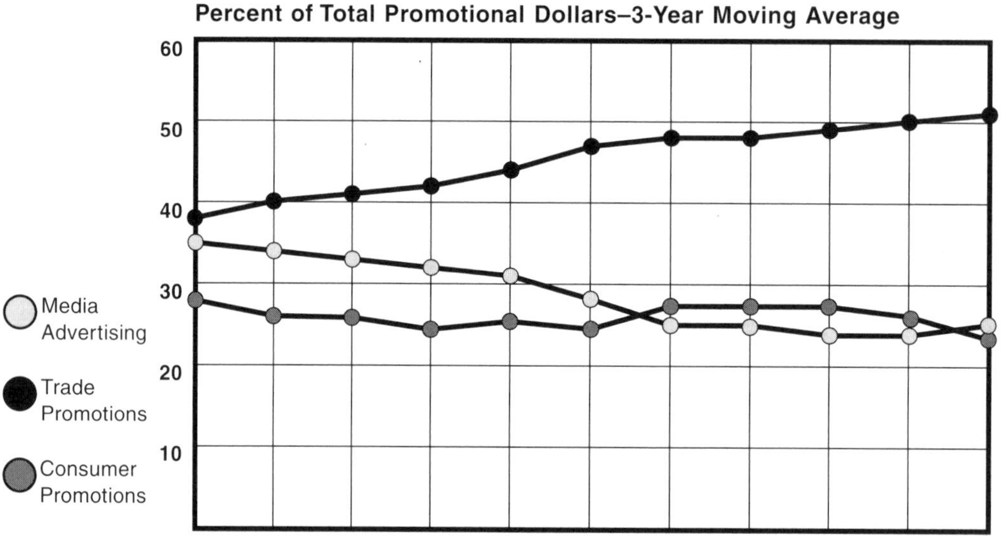

Percent of Total Promotional Dollars–3-Year Moving Average

Year	'85	'86	'87	'88	'89	'90	'91	'92	'93	'94	'95
Media Advertising	35	34	33	32	31	28	25	25	24	24	25
Trade Promotions	38	40	41	42	44	47	48	48	49	50	51
Consumer Promotions	27	26	26	25	26	25	27	27	27	26	24

Source: Annual Surveys of Promotional Practices for 1985–1995.

- Nearly all consumer-products goods companies report using a wide variety of sales promotion techniques. In 1995, 97 percent used coupons, 72 percent used samples, 66 percent used refunds or other money-back offers, 63 percent used sweepstakes, and 56 percent used premium offers.

Why Such Enormous Growth?

The tremendous growth of sales promotion activities among marketers in the United States can be attributed to a number of factors.

- **Sales promotion produces results.** Dollar for dollar, marketers usually get more immediate "bang for their buck" with sales promotion than with any other marketing activity. Sending out a coupon, running a trade deal, or giving a rebate affects consumer and retailer behavior quickly, usually producing a big spike in sales as buyers rush to take advantage of the short-term deal. Most marketing managers have found that if they need a quick sales boost, sales promotion produces results.

- **Sales promotion results occur quickly.** Communications tools such as advertising or public relations are usually perceived as an investment, with sales occurring at some undetermined point in the future. On the other hand, sales promotion usually works during a finite period of time, often showing results within days or even hours. For many marketers who are under increased pressure from management and/or stockholders to get fast results, sales promotion can therefore be very attractive.

- **Sales promotion results are measurable.** Because promotion results in such quick and strong sales, its effects are easy to observe and measure. Therefore sales promotion has generally been viewed as the most scientific tool in the marketing mix. It has been the subject of a large number of efficacy studies by researchers, who in some cases have been able to create formulas predicting exactly how different kinds and amounts of sales promotion will affect sales in different product categories.

- **Sales promotion is relatively easy and inexpensive to implement.** Many marketers today are able to estimate, with a strong degree of accuracy, exactly what will happen to the sales of a brand, and to the sales of its competitors, based on the results of a particular promotion. This has in many cases made promotions easier to design and carry out, and it has allowed companies to move the design of sales promotion activities to lower levels in the management hierarchy, such as assistant brand managers and project-oriented promotion agencies. In addition, sales promotion may be less expensive than other forms of marketing communications. Certainly, the cost of printing coupons, distributing them through free-standing inserts, and reimbursing the retailers who redeem them may often be sizable. On a cost versus results basis, however, sales promotion may be much less expensive than producing and airing television commercials to reach the same audience, especially since the costs of mass media advertising have gone up substantially in recent years.

Problems with Sales Promotions

Obviously, sales promotion has become an increasingly important marketing tool for most U.S. companies. However, this huge growth has led many managers to worry that their firms have begun to rely too much on sales promotion activities. These managers have therefore attempted to reduce their firm's use of promotions or develop promotions that seem more likely to yield positive results. Potential problems with overextensive reliance on sales promotion programs include the following:

- **Many sales promotions are not effective brand-building tools.** Unlike advertising or other forms of consumer communications, many sales promotion activities have little effect on people's attitudes about the product. Therefore, they are unlikely to result in much "residual value"—that is, repeat sales in the future.

- **The overuse of sales promotion activities may have the potential of resulting in less positive attitudes toward the product.** Some researchers argue that if a product is promoted heavily, consumers may assume that the company is unable to sell it at the full price and therefore that the quality must be poor. This phenomenon is more likely to occur in categories where consumers have a hard time judging product quality in other ways—for example, in financial or legal services, vitamins, or film.

- **Even though many sales promotion programs result in a much larger volume of product sold, profitability increases may be relatively low.** This may occur when many people who would have purchased the product anyway take advantage of the promotional offer. In addition, consumers in recent years have become more discriminating with regard to promotions, and often respond only to high-value offers.

- **Sales promotion programs often require substantial implementation costs.** Promotions that result in high sales volume at certain periods create demand for products that is uneven over time, requiring companies to incur the costs of extra production runs or storage costs. Other promotions such as sweepstakes or premiums may require substantial planning and may involve risks that mistakes may be made or that the program may not perform as well as was projected.

- **Sales promotions tend to orient marketing managers toward the short-term.** The ease with which immediate product sales may be manipulated through the use of sales promotion programs may lead some managers to neglect other brand-building activities that, while producing less dramatic short-term results, may lead to more profits over the long run.

Due to these factors, many marketing managers have recently expressed interest in reducing their reliance on sales promotion activities. Simply cutting back on the number of promotions that are run or the amount of money spent on them is likely to produce a less-than-desirable outcome, however, since this strategy will not increase the effectiveness of the promotions that are run and will generally result in decreases in short-term sales. A more optimal approach to the problem is to attempt to use sales promotions strategically, in conjunction with other types of marketing tools, in order to achieve specific goals that will help a product succeed over the long run. This book examines various ways in which sales promotion techniques can be applied using this type of approach.

Redefining Sales Promotion's Role

The traditional definition of sales promotion has been: *Sales promotion gives consumers a short-term incentive to purchase a product.* This definition is accurate, as far as it goes—coupons or value packs or trade deals or other promotions do give consumers more of a reason to purchase a product immediately, and most of these promotions do last for a reasonably short period of time. However, this definition does not state exactly why promotions work nor how they affect the brand from an overall strategic point of view.

To understand how promotions work, it is important to examine the consumer-buying process. Except in the case of very low-involvement, inexpensive, impulse items, most people do not make snap decisions about what products to buy. Instead, they go through a variety of consideration stages before reaching their final decision, including awareness, information gathering, pre-purchase evaluation, decision making, purchase, and post-purchase evaluation.

Different types of marketing activities often work in different ways to affect various aspects of this buying process. Advertising and public relations, for instance, generally affect the awareness, the information gathering, and perhaps the evaluation stages for new products, as consumers learn about products and consider whether or not they might be worth buying. These types of promotions also provide reminders about established products, which may be at parity with other brands. Personal selling may also affect the information-gathering and decision-making stages of the buying process, as the salesperson works to relieve consumers' specific doubts about a product and provides extra encouragement to go ahead and make the purchase.

Sales promotion, however, generally works on a direct behavioral level. Generally, rather than influencing awareness or attitudes—which may or may not eventually translate into corresponding behavior—most types of sales promotions hit directly at the decision-making and purchasing stages of the buying process. This means that while sales promotion usually has less long-term effectiveness than other tactics, it has more immediate results. Sending consumers a coupon for a product they sometimes use, for example, may not change their overall opinion about that product, but it may cause them to purchase it when they ordinarily would not do so.

Sales promotion is able to change behavior directly because it alters the price/value relationship that the product offers the buyer. In some cases this means lowering the price, perhaps with a coupon or rebate or trade deal or on-package price discount. In other cases it means adding something of value to the product—for instance, giving consumers a related item in the package or through a mail-in offer, supplying them with more of the product, or offering them a chance to win a prize in a contest or sweepstakes.

Altering the price/value relationship means that consumers get a better deal and therefore have more of a reason to purchase the product. Moreover, because most promotions last for only a short period of time, consumers have a reason to purchase the product immediately, rather than waiting.

As stated, sales promotion has become increasingly important to U.S. manufacturers. However, although the amount of money that companies spend on sales promotion has grown dramatically, most marketers' overall approach to the field has remained basically the same as it was two decades ago.

Most companies today know that sales promotion is a good way to increase short-term sales and profits. Many sales promotions have become more complex in recent years, often incorporating a variety of promotional elements. In addition, as noted, many marketers and researchers are increasing their attempts to measure the results of sales promotion activities and to conduct them in a more scientific manner.

Nevertheless, the field of sales promotion has in general remained oriented to the short term. In addition, promotions are often not well related to the other strategic elements of the brand's marketing mix. Most of the research into sales promotion has centered on how particular promotions, and levels of promotion, affect short-term sales, not on how those promotions fit into the overall marketing mix and into the overall strategic focus of the company or brand.

As a result, sales promotion is often viewed as a simple, reactionary device in the war to increase immediate sales and profit. Many companies even view sales promotion as no more than a necessary evil—although marketers often wish they could get rid of their promotions or reduce their importance, a mixture of competitive pressures, consumer expectations, and desire for short-term profit often causes those managers to keep investing money in sales promotion.

In short, sales promotion has tended to be a tactically driven discipline. Marketing managers have typically used promotions as short-term volume boosters, often without much analytical thought.

What has generally been missing in the industry is a strategic focus, that is, an examination of how various sales promotion activities affect the overall short-term and long-term positions of the brand in the marketplace. Each category in the market has a different set of dynamics at work within it, and each brand within each category has its own strengths and weaknesses, its own unique positioning and reputation, and its own set of loyal or fickle customers. To be fully effective, sales promotion programs need to recognize all of these factors and be developed in the context of everything else that's happening with a particular brand.

It is therefore appropriate to move to a more strategic definition, one that recognizes sales promotion's role in the overall brand-building process: *Sales promotions are marketing and communications activities that change the price/value relationship of a product or service perceived by the target, thereby (1) generating immediate sales and (2) altering long-term brand value.*

This definition recognizes that sales promotion motivates consumers to purchase a product immediately, either by lowering the price (with the use of coupons, trade discounts, or other means) or by adding value (for instance, with the use of sweepstakes or value packs).

In addition, the definition takes into consideration the concept of a target audience, implying that promotion should be aimed at a specific group of consumers rather than at the population at large. It also recognizes the role of sales promotion in the area of perceived value, suggesting that this is not always a simple matter of concrete attributes and actual price.

Most significantly, the new definition addresses the effect that sales promotion has on the long-term brand value (also known as the brand franchise). The brand franchise is important because it determines how likely consumers are to buy a particular product rather than one of its competitors' products, all else (such as price or distribution) being equal. A stronger brand franchise means that customers are less likely to be affected by competitive promotional activities. In addition, because it means that there is a consumer demand for the product, retailers are more likely to be willing to carry it and possibly to accept a lower margin on it.

Sales promotion does have a residual market value; that is, there may be a long-term effect on the brand franchise after the promotion is over. Sales promotion may also have an effect on the relationship value of the brand, that is, on how positively or negatively consumers feel about a particular product or company.

These types of long-term effects from sales promotion have usually been viewed as negative, with many people believing that too much promotion detracts from the long-term value of the brand. This problem has been particularly prevalent in certain consumer products categories, such as soft drinks or paper and plastic products, where frequent discounting has made the "real" price of the product unclear and has taught consumers and retailers to buy only on deal.

However, depending on the particular situation and goals, sales promotion may also have a positive long-term effect on the brand and on residual market value. The scope of this effect—and whether it occurs—depends on the individual situation, the particular promotion used, and the type of customer targeted.

The rest of this book is designed to help marketers and marketing students to learn to plan sales promotion programs within a more strategic framework. It will examine the kinds of effects that various sales promotion activities have in different situations—in terms of affecting short-term sales before and immediately following the promotion, and in terms of the long-term value of the brand.

CHAPTER TWO

Planning Sales Promotion Programs

Like any other type of marketing activity, sales promotion needs to be evaluated in the context of how it fits into the overall strategy for a particular brand. To be able to conduct promotion activities effectively, it is helpful for marketers to first answer the following questions:

1. *Who are the customers we want to reach?* It is an accepted tenet of marketing that not all customers are alike. In fact, a large percentage of traditional marketing activities is oriented toward segmenting consumers into relevant groups and then determining the appropriate messages to be used to target each group.

Most marketing activities segment consumers according to demographics, psychographics, and other permanent personal characteristics that are assumed to affect the kinds of products that these people are likely to need or desire. Awareness of these personal characteristics is useful in developing products, packaging, advertising, public relations, or other kinds of activities that affect consumer attitudes toward products. Such an awareness is essential to the evaluation of how useful those products are likely to be to them.

As was stated in Chapter 1, however, sales promotion usually works best in affecting behavior, not attitudes. Therefore it makes more sense with sales promotion to segment consumers according to their *behavior*, that is, whether or not they buy the brand, or another product in the category, some or all of the time.

2. *What are the reasons for that behavior?* Just because two people act the same way doesn't necessarily mean that their reasons for doing so are the same. For instance, a person may leave a party early because he is bored, because he is shy, because he hates loud music, because he has a headache, or because he has another engagement. In order to persuade him to stay, it is necessary to understand *why* he's leaving, not just to observe his behavior. We can then take the appropriate action (give him an aspirin, turn down the stereo, or simply let him leave).

The same principle applies to the field of sales promotion. Consumers may choose to purchase or not to purchase a product for a wide variety of reasons. For instance, they may buy a particular brand because they believe it is the best one on the market, because it is less expensive than competitive products, because of habit, or because of a combination of these factors.

It is important to analyze why consumers behave the way they do, because this may affect whether—and how much—they will be influenced by a particular sales promotion program.

3. *What is the goal of the program?* Different sales promotion programs are used for different reasons in order to achieve vastly different ends. For instance, some promotions are designed to achieve consumer trial, with the hope that triers will convert to future buyers. Promotions may be used to match or preempt competitive activities, in order to keep loyal customers from defecting to other products. Some promotions are designed solely to create a short-term sales spike, perhaps to meet the profitability goals of a certain period of time. Obviously, there are many reasons why sales promotion is used—and this needs to be considered in the planning process.

To tie these elements together, it is helpful to introduce a framework that segments consumers into different categories based on their buying behavior.

One commonly used scheme segments consumers of a product category according to whether they are brand loyal (generally using just one brand) or switchers (alternating between two or more brands). According to the model, loyal customers may stockpile (that is, buy products on deal and hoard them for future use) some or all of the time, or they may be classified as not deal prone. Switchers may also be classified as not deal prone (perhaps because they are interested in variety or in meeting different needs with different products), or they may let promotions affect their product choices, perhaps sometimes stockpiling a product when they get a particularly good deal.

Used in a strategic analysis, this model can help promotion managers to better understand their customers. However, it is a bit simplistic in that it assumes consumers either are or are not deal prone. In reality, the dichotomy isn't nearly that complete. Almost all consumers are sometimes influenced by some kind of sales promotion. For instance, a woman who believes that clipping coupons is a waste of time may still purchase a product because of an on-package price reduction or a sweepstakes, and even the most ardent coupon clipper may sometimes buy an attractive product at a high price without a coupon.

Therefore, for the purposes of this book, consumers will be categorized by their typical buying behaviors in the category being examined and by what appears to be causing those behaviors. It then will be possible to choose appropriate promotional techniques to match the specific goals for the brand.

Based on their purchasing behaviors, consumers will be divided into five categories: loyal users of a brand, competitive loyals, switchers, price buyers, and nonusers of the category.

Loyal Users

Loyal users are people who buy a particular brand on a more or less consistent basis. (The term *loyal user* has actually become a relative one in recent years, as fewer consumers have chosen to stick with just one brand. For instance, in some categories, such as toilet tissue, even the most loyal users may buy a particular brand only 60 percent of the time or less. For the purposes of this book, therefore, we will assume that a loyal user is someone who usually, but not necessarily always, buys a particular brand.)

When addressing a company's own loyals, the goal is not to change behavior but to reinforce it, thereby preventing defection and/or increasing current customers' consumption of the brand.

Reinforcing Existing Behavior

In very few cases are consumers unconditionally loyal to a particular product. Instead, they usually make the purchasing decisions they do because of a specific set of factors. They may honestly believe that "their" brand is the best one on the market, or they may think that it's usually a good deal. Habit, or inertia, may also cause them to buy the same product over and over again.

An important point is that loyal consumers can sometimes be won over to competitive products with a change in price, the successful communication of product value, or the simple breaking of consumer habit. Companies may be wise, therefore, to take measures to hold onto their loyal customers with the judicious use of sales promotion programs.

Increased Usage

One good way to improve overall sales is often to increase usage among current customers. Usually this is done by getting a customer to purchase a product when he or she would not ordinarily do so, or to purchase more of the product than usual in the expectation that the extra quantity will be readily consumed. Many consumers who buy an extra-large rather than a large bag of potato chips, for example, will find that the additional amount is easily consumed before the next week's shopping trip.

In other cases, sales promotion may result only in changes in purchase timing among brand loyals, who may take advantage of a good deal and then stockpile the product in the home for future use. A customer who notices bathroom tissue on sale, for instance, may purchase extra to have on hand but probably won't use any additional product just because it's in the house. Therefore future purchases by that customer will probably be curtailed. Changing purchase timing may be an appropriate end in and of itself for some sales promotion programs, however, depending on inventory and manufacturing constraints, the competitive situation, and the financial goals of the brand and the company.

Cross-Selling

Another way to capitalize on brand loyals—or, indeed, on anyone who ever purchases the product—is to attempt to sell them related products. For instance, a skin-care product manufacturer may attempt to sell cleanser to loyal users of its night creams. A doughnut shop may attempt to encourage customers to buy coffee with their regular pastry purchases. These kinds of cross-selling activities may be encouraged by certain types of sales promotion programs.

Competitive Loyals

Competitive loyals are people who use the product category and who usually buy a competitor's brand. There are three basic kinds of consumers who may be brand loyal: intense loyals, value buyers, and those constrained by habit.

Intense Loyals

Consumers may choose a brand because they believe it is the best one on the market, even if it is more expensive than the others. For instance, a woman may always use a certain brand of cosmetics because she thinks that those products are best for her skin. Even in mundane categories such as soft drinks, many consumers are loyal to either Coke or Pepsi, continuing to purchase their favorite even when the competitive brand is much less expensive.

Value Buyers

Consumers may be loyal to a particular brand because it appears to provide the most utility for the cost, even it is not the best one on the market. For instance, if one dishwashing detergent is consistently priced much lower than competitive products but appears to be almost as good in terms of quality, then consumers may purchase it on a regular basis.

Brands may also acquire loyalty because they are of relatively good quality and are affordable. For instance, many consumers might concede that Mercedes is their preferred automobile and that the brand would be worth the cost—if they had the money available. If that isn't the case, they might then repeatedly purchase Toyota or another acceptable but more affordable brand.

Habit-Bound Buyers

Some consumers consistently purchase a brand not because they have made a conscientious study of its perceived value and price in comparison to that of other products on the market, but because it has become their habit to do so.

This type of mentality usually applies to relatively low-involvement products, and it may be more prevalent among consumers who are time-pressed, because it streamlines the buying process. Consumers who buy out of habit have created a simplified decision-making rule that eliminates the need for much thinking—for instance, "If we run out of laundry detergent, buy Tide."

One question here is how consumers originally went about choosing the brand that they now use out of what appears to be habit. Consumers may have started using a particular brand by chance, but they may also have begun using it because they felt that it was actually better than the other products on the market. These original reasons may be difficult to determine, but they may also be important in predicting how susceptible consumers are likely to be to sales promotion programs for other products.

Switchers

Switchers (or "swing users") are people who purchase a variety of brands within a product category. Switchers may be people who use a company's brands as well as competitive ones, or they may be people who use only other companies' products. However, those who switch only among competitive brands are also somewhat like competitive loyals in the way that they must be addressed, as both categories include people who for one reason or another don't currently use a particular brand and probably will be more difficult to convince of its merits.

As brand loyalty has decreased in recent years, the percentage of consumers who can be described as switchers has become a larger part of the population. Addressing switchers has, therefore, become an increasingly important aspect of sales promotion.

People who switch brands may do so for a variety of reasons, or for a combination of those reasons.

Availability

Sometimes people switch brands because their favorite product is not always available at the retail level and they are not willing to go out of their way to find it. For instance, even if a woman is brand loyal to Land O'Lakes margarine, she may not be willing to visit other retailers to find it if it is not carried at the store where she does most of her grocery shopping. Therefore even consumers who are intensely brand loyal may become switchers on certain occasions.

Obviously, availability is a distribution problem. Nevertheless, consumer and retailer promotions may both be used to combat the problem.

Value

Consumers may evaluate the price/value relationship for each brand, or for each product in a set of "acceptable" brands, on each shopping trip, choosing the brand that appears to be the best buy on that particular occasion. Because prices may vary from day to day or from store to store, consumers may buy different brands to fulfill the same need.

Even if consumers strongly prefer a certain brand, they may choose a competitive brand if the price is right. For instance, a person might like Aqua-Fresh toothpaste but may buy Close-Up instead if the price differential is more than 30 cents.

Occasion Usage

Sometimes a consumer may buy different brands within the same category to fulfill different needs or to be consumed on different usage occasions. One classic example of this is the beer drinker who buys Budweiser to consume during the week and Michelob to serve to friends on the weekend. Other studies have shown that consumers may buy softer, decorative toilet tissue for holiday guests, then use the less expensive brands during the rest of the year.

If consumers consistently use the same brand for the same type of usage occasion, however, then they can basically be considered to be brand loyal to that product, since the dynamics are usually the same as with people who are completely brand loyal. To these types of people, it is almost as if there are two totally separate product categories, and they are brand loyal within those categories. They therefore should be addressed as such.

Variety

In some categories and with some consumers, variety is preferred for its own sake. This is a particularly big factor in the breakfast cereal category, where children or adults may tire of eating the same thing morning after morning and choose a variety of products and brands to relieve the monotony. This principle may also be in effect in other categories where many products prevail and where boredom can be a problem, including candy bars, cake mixes, salad dressings, and—as people transfer their own desire for variety to their perception of what their cats and dogs want—pet food.

Price Buyers

Some consumers purchase brands solely on the basis of price. These customers may consistently purchase one brand if it is always the least expensive one in the marketplace, or they may switch among brands if some products vary in price across time. For instance, price buyers may consistently buy generic spaghetti sauce, unless one of the nationally advertised brands has a particularly good deal and matches the generic's price.

Price buyers generally either have little disposable income and can't afford to purchase the more expensive products or attach little importance to the differences between brands. For instance, some purchasers of flour believe that all brands are exactly the same, and therefore they always purchase the least expensive one. Most advertising and other image-building promotional techniques are designed to alter this view and make one brand appear to be more desirable than others, thereby removing the commodity image and increasing the price that consumers will be willing to pay for certain brands.

In most categories in the United States, price buyers tend to be a minor, but growing, percentage of the population. There is evidence that price buyers in a category are often heavy users of that category, however. The fact that they buy so much of the product may account for the reason that they are so price sensitive.

Nonusers

Nonusers are people who don't currently use any product in a particular category. Their failure to do so may be attributed to several factors.

Price

Some people would like to purchase a particular type of product but can't afford to do so. For instance, many people may wish they had their own helicopters to commute quickly back and forth from work, but they do not have enough money to make the investment.

Value

In some cases people don't buy a certain type of product because they believe it to be overpriced. For instance, some people refuse to buy convenience products like gourmet frozen dinners because they think they are too expensive and not worth the money.

Lack of Need

In some cases consumers may believe that the use of a particular product will not improve their lives, or they may in fact have absolutely no need for that product. For instance, some people don't use mouthwash because they don't think they need it. People without young children obviously have no reason to purchase diapers or baby car seats, no matter how attractive a deal they get on them.

In summary, consumers may behave in different ways for widely divergent reasons. Although these categorizations of usual buying behaviors may appear to be a little obvious, they can be helpful in segmenting consumers for the development of various kinds of sales promotion programs.

Incidentally, none of these classifications should be considered absolute. In many categories, consumers may move in and out of different classifications, perhaps moving from brand loyalty to a particular product to becoming a switcher to dropping out of the category. However, what is particularly important is not the behavior of any individual consumer, but the general tendencies of the population as a whole. These can be gauged by marketers through a wide variety of research techniques.

Once marketers understand the dynamics occurring in a particular category at a specific point in time, they can then choose the appropriate promotional programs to best contribute to the specific goals they want to achieve.

CHAPTER THREE

Selecting the Appropriate Promotional Tools

Once marketers understand the dynamics occurring within their product category and have determined the particular consumers and consumer behaviors they want to influence, they can then go about using various promotional techniques to achieve those goals.

As the promotional techniques are discussed, it is important to realize that each can produce impressive immediate results in most categories and for most brands. This is the way that many marketers view promotional tools—as a sure way to achieve a certain amount of sales over a particular period in time.

However, it is important to realize that not all promotions work in the same way. For example, certain sales promotions are extremely effective at changing the behaviors of one type of consumer but may do nothing to affect another type. In addition, while some sales promotions may increase the value of the brand over the long run by making consumers more willing to buy the product at a higher price, other promotions may leave the long-term value of the brand unchanged or may even decrease it. Before conducting promotional programs, therefore, it is crucial that marketers take a hard look at the dynamics currently occurring in the category, including the percentage of the population that engages in each of the purchase behaviors, the reasons for those behaviors, and the changes that are currently occurring in the marketplace.

Exhibit 3.1 Types of Consumers and Sales Promotion
Results Desired

Type	Description	Desired Results
Current Loyals	People who buy the "right" product most or all of the time.	Reinforce behavior, increase consumption, change purchase timing.
Competitive Loyals	People who buy a competitor's product most or all of the time.	Break loyalty, persuade to switch to promoted brand.
Switchers	People who buy a variety of products in the category.	Persuade to buy the "right" brand more often.
Price Buyers	People who consistently buy the least expensive brand.	Entice with low prices or supply added value that makes price less important.
Nonusers	People who don't use any product in the category.	Create awareness of category and product, persuade that product is worth buying.

After they determine the general characteristics of the marketplace and decide on the objectives they want to accomplish, marketers can go about designing the promotional programs that will best help them to reach these goals.

This chapter covers some broad principles concerning the kinds of sales promotions that are appropriate to effectively target different kinds of consumers. Each of these techniques is described more thoroughly in the rest of the book; the discussion here is intended to tie them together and show some of the alternative ways in which different consumers may be influenced. This chapter also covers the effects different types of promotions can have on long-term sales and the brand franchise.

Consumer Segments and Sales Promotion Techniques

The various consumer segments described in Chapter 2 generally react differently to different sales promotion techniques.

Loyal Users

When companies look at consumers who are more or less loyal to their brands (*loyal* meaning that they purchase the desired product a large percentage of or all of the time and have relatively positive feelings toward it), they will not want to *change behavior*. Rather, they need to reinforce that behavior, increase product usage, or expand upon current product usage.

Reinforcing Behavior

By reinforcing loyal customers' present behavior, companies attempt to prevent them from being lured away by competitors' promotional activities. In doing this, marketers find it helpful to give those consumers some extra reason to stick with the brand.

One way to accomplish this is through continuity programs. Since loyal customers intend to buy the brand in the future, they probably will be willing to sign up for continuity programs. Once signed up, they may be more resistant to the promotional efforts of other brands. Cause-related promotions may make some loyals feel good about purchasing the product and therefore less inclined to defect. "Extras" (such as bonus packs, sweepstakes, specialty packages, or premiums) may also serve to enhance the perceived value of the brand and make the consumer believe that it is a good choice.

Price promotions are of more limited value in reinforcing behavior. Loyals will certainly be willing to take advantage of coupons or discounts, but it is unlikely that these activities will increase their brand loyalty in the future; in fact, some studies show that too-frequent discounting may even hurt the image of the brand among loyal consumers. Nevertheless, some price promotions may be necessary in certain cases simply to counter competitive activities and prevent core users from being lured away to other products.

Increasing Usage

A good way to capitalize on current users of a brand is to persuade them to purchase additional product. This product may be immediately consumed or it may be stockpiled for future use. Whether the product is used immediately depends on a variety of factors, such as the type of product being used, how much is already being consumed, and whether the product can replace others currently being used. Ice cream bars, for instance, may be consumed easily by consumers who want snacks, whereas toothpaste consumption may have no potential for increasing. On the basis of their experiences with the product, most managers can predict relatively easily how quickly the extra product sold to current customers will be used up.

In some cases, too, simply shifting purchasing timing to the present may be beneficial in and of itself. Sometimes this may help companies to meet the profitability or sales goals of a particular period in time; at other times getting consumers to purchase extra product will mean that they will be less likely to buy a competitive brand in the near future.

Most sales promotion techniques can, at least at times, be successful in persuading current customers to increase their purchases of products. Probably the most direct method is through bonus packs, which give consumers an incentive to stock up. Price promotions may be successful in getting people to buy more product than they might ordinarily; whether this results in overall increased volume over time depends, as stated, on the overall behavioral dynamics of the category.

Continuity plans also may result in increased purchases, as consumers strive to acquire enough "points" to obtain the desired reward. (This may not be an effective tool in some situations where the product is high-priced or infrequently needed, however. For instance, frequent flyer programs are unlikely to encourage most people to fly more, since the cost of each flight is so high. Instead, frequent flyer programs tend to work best in creating loyalty among travelers who would otherwise switch from airline to airline.)

Interest-generating promotions such as bonus packs, specialty packaging, premiums, and point-of-purchase materials may also succeed in selling additional product to current users. Sweepstakes or contests can also be successful in certain circumstances, particularly when entry can be tied to product usage. For instance, McDonald's has experienced strong increased volume with its sweepstakes promotions, which require consumers to visit a restaurant to pick up a game piece.

Cross-Selling

Promotions may be used to sell additional, different products to current customers. For instance, coupons for other brands may be included in product packaging, or bonus packs may offer free samples of the secondary item. Two or more related items have also been tied together in sweepstakes, rebate, or premium offers.

Competitive Loyals

Competitive loyals are obviously a tough group to win over. In many cases, these consumers are particularly predisposed toward their current brand, and they may not be willing to consider other products. In addition, these people have undoubtedly been hit with promotions for competitive brands in the past, and they have been generally unaffected by them. It is therefore likely that most ordinary promotions will continue to be ineffective.

Intense Loyals

The conversion of competitive loyals is a particularly big problem with people who are truly convinced of a particular brand's merits and who are psychologically committed to that brand. For these people, it is almost as though other brands in the category do not even exist; they are therefore likely to be immune to sales promotion activities. One exception might be sampling, which could introduce some intense loyals to the superior qualities of a competitive product. This will produce sales, however, only when the sampled brand has not been tried before and when it is noticeably superior in some way to the one currently being used.

Value Seekers

Competitive loyals who believe that "their" brand is generally the best *buy* on the market (but not necessarily the best-quality product) are not quite as resistant to sales promotion as are intense loyals, but they are nevertheless likely to be tough sells. Probably the best tool, again, is sampling, but only for brands that have not yet been tried and that have some obvious advantage over the currently used brand. Other sales promotion tools—high-value coupons, attractive sweepstakes, specialty packaging, bonus packs—may also be somewhat effective in certain circumstances, depending on how much value they appear to bring to the brand and on the consumer's attitude toward the product being promoted. Perhaps the main problem here is simply getting loyal customers to notice and consider promotions for brands they don't use, since they usually do not pay attention to materials concerning other brands.

Habit-Bound Buyers

Getting consumers to notice the promotion is also a key issue when inertia is a problem; however, once these consumers who buy from habit do notice the competitive brand, making a sale may be much easier than with other loyals. Sampling may be particularly effective in persuading consumers who buy out of habit, providing that the quality of the brand being promoted is superior and noticeable. Other promotions that create consumer interest may also be useful, including sweepstakes, bonus packs, specialty packaging, and premiums. What usually do not work are price promotions, as inertia buyers usually aren't even looking at price, although a particularly high-value coupon may catch the attention of a few of these consumers.

It is worth noting that in the case of consumers who are currently brand loyal because of inertia, the method of promotion delivery may be just as important, or even more important, than the type of sales promotion used. Because these consumers are not looking for sales promotions and may also be time-pressed, it may be necessary to catch their attention through some kind of unusual delivery system or creative approach. It also may be the case, however, that some consumers who buy brands out of inertia, if persuaded to try a competitive product, may begin to buy the new brand out of habit in the future. It therefore may prove to be worthwhile to put extra effort into winning over those customers.

Switchers

Switchers or swing users are people who purchase a variety of brands within one category. In general, switchers are much easier to win over with sales promotions than are competitive loyals, as they have purchased a variety of products in the past. However, it may also be the case that since switchers attach less importance to their brand choice, they are not very likely to stick with a particular brand after the promotion is over.

Availability

In certain cases consumers may switch brands because their preferred brand is not readily available. Getting distribution is certainly a difficult issue, and it is one that relies on a variety of factors, such as product mix, previous manufacturer success ratios, manufacturer support for the product, and available retail space. Sales promotion activities do not provide a complete solution to the distribution issue; nevertheless, they may sometimes be helpful in gaining distribution at the retail level.

Exhibit 3.2 Type of Sales Promotions

Type	Description
Coupon	Certificate allowing consumer to get reduced price at purchase.
Bonus Pack	More product for the regular price.
In-Pack On-Pack, Near-Pack	Gift given to consumers at purchase.
Specialty Container	Container that can be reused or that adds value to the product.
Continuity Program	Reward system for multiple purchases.
Refund	Consumer gets money back after purchase.
Sweepstakes	Consumer has a random chance to win a prize—no purchase required.
Contest	Consumers compete to win a prize—purchase may be required.
Through-the-Mail Premium	Gift given to consumers after the purchase.
Sampling	Product is given to consumers for free.
Price-Off	Product package informs consumer that marked price is lower than regular price.
Trade Deal	Retailer gets discount on price of product or incentive for promoting the product to consumers.
Cause-Related Promotion	Donation to charitable organization is made by company for each unit of product sold.

Trade deals, though reducing the manufacturer margin, may be effective in persuading retailers that it is worth their while to stock a particular brand. Coupons, sampling, sweepstakes, and continuity plans—because they create consumer demand and cause consumers to look for the product (and perhaps complain when it's not available)—may also be helpful in certain circumstances.

However, price-offs, refunds, bonus packs, and other promotions that consumers find out about in-store will not usually create consumer demand or increase distribution, since if the brands and promotions are not in the store, consumers have no way of learning about them. And specialty packaging—which may in some cases be odd-sized and difficult to fit on a store shelf or in the warehouse—may actually detract from the chance of getting good distribution.

Value Buyers

Often when consumers switch back and forth among different brands, it is because they are not particularly committed to any of them and simply choose the one that appears to be the best deal at the time from all products in the category or from a set of preselected brands. Although they may prefer certain brands over others, those considerations are outweighed by price some or all of the time.

Because these consumers are interested in value, promotions that lower the price of the brand may be very effective at increasing sales over the short term among this group. These may include coupons (provided that the consumer in question clips coupons), rebates, trade deals, price-offs, or bonus packs. Continuity programs may also be effective in some cases, depending on the perceived value of the item being saved for, since they directly address the habit of switching and give consumers a reward for sticking with one brand.

Other promotions that bring some kind of added value to the brand may also be effective, depending on their desirability. Promotions of this type may include sweepstakes, bonus packs, specialty packaging, and premiums. Point-of-purchase (POP) materials may also be of some use, especially for impulse products, in that they call attention to a particular brand and cause consumers to examine it more closely. (Because consumers may still be looking for value, however, it may be most effective to pair POP materials with another type of promotion, such as a price-off or specialty package, for maximum effectiveness.)

Sampling probably will not provide much motivation to these customers, unless they have never tried a particular brand before.

Occasion Usage

One of the reasons that consumers may buy different brands within a category is to fulfill discrete needs. For instance, a woman may consistently buy Diet Coke for herself and Mountain Dew for her husband. If these choices are truly consistent, then these consumers should probably be viewed as brand loyal, and treated as described in the sections on competitive loyals or loyal users.

Variety Seekers

Consumers who switch from one brand to another may have variety as a goal, perhaps in combination with value. Variety is a particularly important issue in many food product categories, where people may get bored with eating the same thing over and over again. It may also be a factor in other industries, such as personal products (fragrances and shampoos, for example) or fashion.

Variety seekers benefit from buying a number of different products. Therefore the goal of sales promotion programs should be to provide the consumer with an incentive to purchase the brand some of the time or at a particular point in time. The good news here is that because these people are interested in having a selection of brands, they may be easily swayed by sales promotion efforts that tip the scales toward a particular brand. By the same token, they are also likely to be easily influenced by promotional efforts for competitive brands, and they probably will not stay with any product after a particular promotion is over.

Consumers who are interested in variety are likely to exhibit a strong positive reaction to most types of sales promotion programs. Price promotions (either in-store or through coupons) are likely to elicit large amounts of increased sales from those variety seekers who are price sensitive. Promotions that add extra value to the brand and make it appear more fun may also be useful— sweepstakes and contests, bonus packs, specialty packaging, and premiums are all good examples of this tendency. Point-of-purchase materials, because they attract the consumer's attention to the brand, may also be effective. Probably the only types of programs that would be considered generally ineffective at reaching this kind of consumer would be continuity programs (since consumers desiring variety would not want to commit themselves to one product) and sampling (because consumers may have already tried most of the brands on the market).

Price Buyers

Price buyers are people who consistently purchase the lowest-priced brand on the market. This may mean that they consistently buy one brand, if it is always the least expensive, or they may switch among brands as prices change.

Price buyers may be affected by price promotions, but only if the promotions reduce the price of the brand to match that of the competitive brand that would have been purchased instead. This can generally be accomplished through coupons, price-offs, refunds, or trade deals that are passed on to the consumer. Other promotions that add value, such as bonus packs, continuity plans, specialty packaging, premiums, and extra product may occasionally be successful in winning these customers, but they generally are much less effective.

Because these consumers are looking solely at price, they will purchase the brand only during the promotion. After the promotion, they nearly always will return to whatever other brand is the cheapest.

Nonusers

Nonusers are people who don't use any product in the category. As such, they are particularly resistant to most sales promotion activities.

One of the reasons that sales promotions work so poorly at affecting nonusers of a product category is that these types of people generally have negative attitudes about the category as a whole. Before sales promotion can work to influence behavior, it is necessary to change those negative attitudes, perhaps with the use of advertising, personal selling, public relations, or positive word of mouth.

Price Problems

In a few cases, especially with high-cost items, nonusers might want to purchase a product but simply find it too expensive. In those cases it is possible to use price promotions to increase sales, but only if the price discounts are substantial. For instance, Jaguar might attract a number of nonusers of luxury automobiles if it offered a $10,000 rebate on each car purchased. However, since this kind of discounting cuts substantially into profit margins, most companies are willing to do it only in extreme circumstances.

Value

Some people could afford to purchase a particular type of product but don't think that it's worth the price. Sampling may sometimes cause these people to reconsider a product's value, if they haven't tried a particular brand before; they may also, in a few select circumstances, take advantage of a large price discount or a particularly attractive peripheral offer, such as a sweepstakes or specialty package or premium. However, again, since these people have failed to use the product in the past, they probably will be unmoved by most promotions for items in that category.

Lack of Need

Some nonusers either may perceive that they really don't need a particular type of product or may actually have no use whatsoever for it. Consumers who see no value in a particular product may occasionally be persuaded otherwise with the use of a sample, but this is relatively rare. And people who actually have no use for a product (for instance, people without lawns do not need lawn mowers) will certainly be uninfluenced by any type of sales promotion.

Using the Behavior Analysis Model

In planning a more strategic sales promotion program, marketers will do well to first investigate the overall pattern of consumption in the category and the relative position of each of the customer groups within that category. For instance, in some categories nearly all customers are switchers, while in others many consumers stick with one particular brand. In other categories, particularly those that are in the growth stage, a large percentage of the population may be nonusers but nonetheless have some potential for future consumption.

It is also important to look at each brand individually. For instance, a widely recognized brand may work to capitalize on the goodwill of its brand loyal customers, whereas a relatively unknown brand that is trying to grow may need to focus most of its attention on stealing share from switchers or competitive loyals. In some categories, such as laundry detergent, a percentage of consumers may be loyal to one particular brand, while others swing back and forth between two or more brands. Understanding what is going on in the marketplace is the first step toward using sales promotion to achieve specific goals. This type of information is increasingly available through scanner data provided by such companies as Information Resources Inc. (IRI) and A.C. Nielsen.

The second step is to try to understand why consumers behave the way they do. For instance, consumers who never buy a particular brand because they believe that it is of poor quality should not be expected to purchase it just because the manufacturer drops a high-value coupon for it. In order to change those consumers' behavior, the marketer will first need to change their attitudes, perhaps through product reformulation, advertising, public relations, or a sampling program. On the other hand, consumers who fail to buy a brand because they have forgotten about it, because they think it's too expensive, or because they have grown used to buying a different brand may be appropriate targets for the right sales promotion programs. This kind of information about the market as a whole must generally be gathered through some sort of qualitative research, such as a focus group, survey, in-depth interview, or observational study.

The third step is to determine the types of promotional activities that competitors have begun or are planning and the effects these activities are likely to have on the marketplace. Knowledge of competitive activities in the areas of product development, advertising, sales promotion, packaging, public relations, trade activities, and geographic targeting can be acquired by observing the marketplace, monitoring trade publications, keeping in touch with retailers, carefully examining scanner data for changes in trends, and simply imagining what actions competitors are likely to take based on their current management, financial constraints, and the situation in the marketplace. Scanner data from past promotions can enable marketers to predict what effects specific competitive activities are likely to have on the marketplace. Armed with this information, marketers will be better prepared to use sales promotion or other tools to effectively counter those activities.

The fourth step in planning a sales promotion program is to determine the program's goals—that is, to determine whether the program is designed to increase profits over the short term or the long term and which types of consumers are to be targeted. Many sales promotion programs are successful either at increasing the long-term potential of the brand or at producing short-term profits, but not both. Thus it is important to determine what the purpose of a particular sales promotion effort is supposed to be. Marketers should also decide what types of consumers (such as loyal users, switchers, competitive loyals, or nonusers of the category) need to be targeted, and which types of sales promotion tactics will work best to accomplish the desired goals.

In short, this book is not designed to provide marketers with "rules" about how to use sales promotions, because every situa-

Exhibit 3.3 Types of Consumers and Appropriate Promotions

Consumer Types		Coupons	Special Packs	Sampling	Contests/ Sweepstakes	Continuity Programs	Refunds	Price-Offs/ Discounts	Premiums	Trade Deals	Cause-Related Promotions
CURRENT LOYALS	Reinforced	Strong	Strong	Limited	Strong	Strong	Strong	Strong	Strong	Strong	Strong
	Extra Sales	Moderate	Strong	None	Strong (depends)	Strong	Moderate	Strong	Moderate	Strong	Moderate
	Crossover Sales	Moderate	Strong	—	Strong (depends)	Strong	Moderate	—	Strong	—	Limited
COMPETITIVE LOYALS	Intense Loyals	None	None	Limited	Limited	None	None	None	Limited	None	Limited
	Value Seekers	Limited	Limited	Moderate	Limited	Limited	Limited	None	Limited	Limited	Limited
	Inertia	Limited	Limited	Strong	Strong	Moderate	Limited	None	Moderate	Limited	Strong
SWITCHERS	Value	Strong	Strong	None	Strong	Strong	Strong	Strong	Strong	Strong	Strong
	Variety	Strong	Strong	None	Strong	None	Strong	Strong	Strong	Strong	Strong
	Distribution	Moderate	None	Strong	Limited	Moderate	Limited	None	None	Moderate	Moderate
PRICE BUYERS		Strong	Limited	Limited	Limited	Limited	Strong	Limited	Limited	Strong	None
NON-USERS	Price	Limited	None	None	None	None	Moderate	None	None	Limited	None
	Value	Limited	None	Limited	Limited	Limited	Moderate	None	Limited	Limited	Limited
	Lack of Need	None	None	None	None	None	None	None	None	None	None

◯ = positive residual value may be created

tion is different and therefore will require individual understanding and planning. Instead, it is intended to give some generalized theories on how specific sales promotion tactics work and on when they tend to be most appropriate. Armed with that information and with knowledge of the specific situation confronting a particular brand, marketers will then be able to create programs individually tailored to their particular needs.

Other Issues Pertaining to the Behavioral Analysis Model

A model such as the one described may seem, at least on paper, simple to understand and use. It may even appear that all marketers need to do is determine the type of customers they want to reach, and then conduct the appropriate promotional activities to reach those targets.

However, the model—and the field of sales promotion—is not that simplistic. Therefore it is important to recognize the stumbling blocks that marketers may face when conducting sales promotion activities.

One issue is that consumer behavior in most categories is generally in a state of flux. Individual consumers may move in and out of different categories as their needs or lifestyles change. (To take two obvious examples, a man may start clipping coupons when he loses his job, and nonusers of diapers will start buying them when they have children.) In addition, the composition of behaviors in the entire category may change, due to changes in lifestyles, the economy, competition, or other factors. Therefore marketers need to carefully monitor the marketplace in order to keep up-to-date on any changes that might be occurring.

Another major problem is that sales promotions aimed at one segment of the marketplace will often be seen and, perhaps, used by everyone in the market. In many cases this does not matter; in other cases, however, excessive redemption of the promotion by the wrong group may nullify any positive immediate profits. Probably the most common example of this is when marketers use high-value coupons or other price promotions to try to lure competitive users to try their brands, in the hope that they will purchase them again in the future. What often happens is that few competitive users take advantage of the coupons, while many, many current users (most of whom might have purchased the products anyway) redeem them. This kind of issue is slowly being addressed by new forms of consumer targeting and distribution such as direct marketing; nevertheless, it remains a crucial issue.

Finally, sales promotion can be especially effective when it is integrated with other types of marketing activities, especially those that affect consumer attitudes, such as product changes, advertising, or public relations. For example, a new or reformulated brand that addresses competitive loyals in advertising by describing the product advantages may benefit from using sales promotion, such as coupons, to encourage purchasing. Therefore, when developing their sales promotion programs, marketers need to be careful to consider everything that is happening with their own brands as well as with competitive products.

The Issue of Payout

Another crucial point in the use of promotional techniques is the widespread belief that the individual promotion, because its effects tend to be short term, must provide increased profits during the life of the promotion.

Because this book is intended to be an overview of the field of sales promotion, the complicated and technical issues of how to estimate payout will not be covered here in an in-depth fashion. Nevertheless, most marketers who conduct sales promotion programs do look at the issue of payout, and so its value and limitations should be understood.

Basically, payout means that promotional programs have resulted in increased profits *in the time period during and immediately following the promotion*. The cost of the promotion is compared with the extra profits generated by the incremental value due to the promotional activity.

In order to predict payout, it is first necessary to estimate the profits that would have been made during a period of time if the promotion hadn't been run. The period of time measured usually includes the time during the promotion as well as some length of time following it, for the reason that promotions usually "cannibalize" future sales because consumers tend to stock up on promoted items and therefore may not need to purchase them again for a while. (This effect may even be seen in industries where consumers cannot stock up on the item; for instance, people who have visited Burger King several times in one week may tire of the food and not want to eat there again for a while.)

In certain cases, too, especially when promotional periods can be predicted by consumers, the time period *before* the promotion occurs may be examined. This is because if consumers can predict that a promotion may occur, they may wait to buy the product. For instance, some consumers may realize that Coca-Cola goes on special every few weeks in one store or another, and they may therefore buy only a minimal amount of the product until they can get it on deal. Other people may realize that certain department store cosmetics counters have "bonus days" every season, and they may wait for those times to purchase needed items. The length of the time period that must be examined varies from category to category, and it is dependent on ordinary purchase behaviors and on the perishability and bulkiness of the product.

Once the "regular" profits are estimated, they should be compared with the anticipated profits of the same period of time if the promotion is run. Increasingly, this number can be accurately predicted by using mathematical models derived from previous brand activities. Although these types of models can be fairly complicated, they usually take into consideration the type, amount, and length of the promotion, as well as other relevant factors.

Obviously, sales promotions involve trade-offs. In the case of price promotions, increased volume is paired with decreased profit margin. With other promotions, such as sweepstakes, increased volume is countered by the overhead (or fixed costs) of the sales promotion. Therefore each promotion needs to be analyzed beforehand to determine if it really appears to be worthwhile. Promotions should also be evaluated after they are over, to make certain that they did indeed pay out.

The reason that payout is so important in the field of sales promotion is that results of promotions are often assumed to be short term. In contrast with advertising and other activities that affect attitudes and that may therefore influence sales far into the future, the behavior-oriented discipline of sales promotion is often assumed to have no long-term effects. Therefore profits must be gained now or never.

This generalization is much too bold, however. There are several cases when sales promotion *can* affect long-term sales and can change the residual market value and relationship value of the brand. When this is the case, immediate payout may not always be necessary, as the following examples illustrate.

1. Sampling may convince people of a brand's merits, and because of this attitude change these consumers may continue to buy the product over and over again in the future. Therefore sampling is rarely expected to show immediate payout.

Instead, it is usually considered one of the expenses of launching a brand, similar to advertising or slotting allowances (the one-time fee that manufacturers pay retailers for adding a product to their distribution).

2. Certain promotions, such as high-value coupons or other price promotions, may cause consumers to try brands that they have never used before. If this occurs and consumers' attitudes are favorably influenced, then that promotion will have created long-term value.

3. Sometimes people may change their behavior because of a promotion, then stick with that brand out of inertia. This means that long-term value has been created, because consumers are continuing to buy the product without additional promotion. (The frequency of this kind of occurrence is uncertain, however; more research needs to be done on this topic.)

4. Sometimes promotion may reinforce current loyals' behavior and keep them from trying other brands in the face of competitive promotion. This theory assumes that consumers who try competitive brands may continue to use those products in the future. If a manufacturer's own promotion can keep its loyal customers from trying those other products, then those people may be more likely to stick with their current brand in the future. (Again, it is not known exactly how often this particular scenario occurs.)

5. Promotion may sometimes persuade a retailer to stock a particular brand or to reconsider discontinuing it. For instance, if many consumers attempt to use a coupon for a brand or if the retailer gets a big trade deal, increased distribution that will continue even after the promotion is over may be gained.

6. Occasionally consumers may get used to buying a larger size or more containers of a brand during a promotional period. If that product is easily consumed, the larger amount may continue to be purchased on a regular basis even after the promotion is over. For instance, consider a woman who usually buys one 12-pack of Pepsi Cola for her family per week. If one week a 24-pack is on sale and if the family easily consumes it by the end of the week, she may decide to purchase a 24-pack every week in to the future. (Again, it's uncertain how often this trade-up behavior occurs.)

7. Sometimes a promotion may result in actual improved customer feeling about a brand. For instance, an interesting sweepstakes may result in long-term awareness and goodwill, particularly if the consumer wins some sort of prize. Consumers using a coupon may attend more thoughtfully to the selling message accompanying it in the newspaper than they do to other advertising, such as television commercials. Premiums (say, a Budweiser beach towel) may act as long-term reminders and goodwill builders. Certainly, event and cause-related marketing may result in positive consumer awareness and attitudes, which may translate into long-term sales.

8. Companies that engage in frequent price discounting may find that their long-term brand value may deteriorate due to the promotion. This may be because consumers start to view the discounted price as the "real" price and become unwilling to pay the full regular price in the future. (A case in point is the airline industry, where discounts have taught consumers that they should always avoid paying full price.) Some researchers also theorize that consumers may look at a brand that's always on deal and wonder what's wrong with the product, decreasing the value of the brand.

Because sales promotion activities may have these types of effects on the long-term success of brands, marketers should weigh all of their implications when planning promotional programs. Looking only at short-term profits can cause marketers to miss some of the long-term advantages or liabilities inherent in their programs.

CHAPTER FOUR

Coupons

Couponing is by far the most popular and relied-upon form of consumer sales promotion in the United States. Approximately 292 billion manufacturer-originated coupons were distributed in the United States in 1995, amounting to almost 3,000 coupons per household. Manufacturers spent about $8 billion in 1995 on distributing, handling and redeeming coupons, with almost all major grocery and health-and-beauty manufacturers using coupons to at least some extent for their marketing programs. About 5.8 billion total coupons (or an average of about 80 per household) were redeemed by consumers, with more than 80 percent of individuals admitting to using coupons at least occasionally.

Although coupons are likely to remain an extremely important promotional tool for marketers in the future, there has been some movement in recent years to change the way and the extent to which they are used. For example, the number of coupons distributed by manufacturers decreased by about 6 percent from 1994 to 1995, with many companies stating that they intended to reduce coupon usage even further in the future.

Manufacturer interest in reducing coupon usage can be attributed to a number of factors, including declining redemption rates from consumers deluged with coupons and the realization through the analysis of scanner data that many coupon sales are made to consumers who would have purchased the product anyway.

Exhibit 4.1   Billions of Coupons Distributed

1985	199.9	1991	292.0
1986	225.2	1992	310.0
1987	238.3	1993	298.5
1988	247.4	1994	309.7
1989	267.6	1995	291.9
1990	279.4	1996	268.5

Source: NCH **Promotional Services.**

Although coupons may be used slightly less frequently in the future, it seems likely that they will continue to be an important part of most companies' marketing programs.

Coupons have often been thought of as certificates that entitle the consumer to some sort of incentive to buy a product. Although that incentive is usually a reduction in the price of the product at the retail level, coupons can also be used to deliver refunds, combination offers, free samples, or other types of promotions.

Coupons are generally divided into two basic types: (1) trade-originated and (2) manufacturer-originated. Trade-originated coupons are redeemable only at a particular store or group of stores. They are designed to get consumers to shop at that retail outlet and preferably to purchase impulse items when inside.

Manufacturer-originated coupons, on the other hand, are distributed by the maker or marketer of the product. They usually may be redeemed at any retailer that carries the product; the retailer then receives reimbursement for the face value of the coupons plus a handling fee.

Although most of this chapter will concentrate on manufacturer-originated coupons, much of this discussion—including distribution channels and consumer buying behavior—can also be applied to those that are trade-originated. Trade coupons will be discussed further in Chapter 13.

Consumer Usage

What type of person uses coupons? Perhaps the best answer would simply be "Everybody." About 83 percent of Americans use coupons at least some of the time (compared to 77 percent in 1990 and only 58 percent in 1971), and usage tends to be fairly independent of age, income, education, lifestyle, race, and gender. Psychographic and shopping-related characteristics are sometimes thought to be better predictors of coupon usage than demographics, although it is difficult for marketers to obtain this kind of information in order to target specific individuals with coupon offers. People who are more likely to use coupons include those who are not especially busy, who see themselves as "smart" or comparison shoppers, and who take great pride in their homemaking abilities.

Although most individuals use coupons occasionally, only about 27 percent of U.S. consumers state that they use coupons every time they shop. In general, women tend to use coupons more frequently than men do, but that is probably because women do routine shopping more frequently.

Heavy users of coupons are more likely to have children, to have high grocery bills, and to live in the suburbs. They are more likely than the overall population to be retired or full-time homemakers, probably because collecting and organizing coupons can take a significant amount of time. Finally, heavy coupon users are relatively likely to live in markets where retailers frequently offer double- or triple-couponing programs (that is, two or three times the face value of coupons up to a certain amount), since this makes the effort of clipping coupons especially worthwhile.

Evidence suggests that consumers are more likely to use coupons during a recession or when they personally are worried about their economic future. This tendency may again tie in with the so-called "smart-shopper syndrome," since people who are anxious about their financial future may gain some sense of control when they save money, no matter how small the amount or how large their current income.

Prevalence of Coupon Usage

Coupons have increased in popularity among marketers of consumer products for a number of reasons:

- Coupons provide a means of distributing a price cut to consumers, who have become increasingly price sensitive and less brand loyal.

- Unlike regular price cuts, coupons may make consumers feel that they are getting a good deal on a particular product, thereby causing them to increase consumption.

- Also unlike regular price cuts, coupons provide temporary

price reductions; the brand returns to the regular price after the expiration date.

- Coupons may encourage new consumers to try a product, increasing the value of the brand over the long run.

- Coupons ensure that price cuts are passed on to the consumer. (Often, retailers who receive a decrease in their wholesale price of a product may absorb it as extra margin rather than reducing the retail price on the shelf and passing the savings on to the consumer.)

- Coupons may be effective in differentiating between price-sensitive and price-insensitive consumers. Those who are price sensitive are assumed to be more likely to clip coupons, whereas those who don't care very much about how much the product costs are more likely to pay full price.

- Coupon distribution may now be easily targeted to particular areas of the country or particular types of consumers, helping companies to accomplish specific targeted marketing goals.

- Coupons may encourage consumers to demand the product at the store level, making it more likely that the retailer will begin or continue to carry the couponed product.

- Consumers who are not particularly price-sensitive may use coupons to make purchasing decisions. This may be especially true of people who feel they don't have time to compare shelf prices on a number of different products, but who still want to feel as if they are saving money.

The issue of influencing the retailer through the use of coupons is an especially important one for manufacturers of groceries and of health and beauty products—by far the most frequent users of this type of sales promotion. These kinds of manufacturers in recent years have held decreasing power in comparison to retailers, who may legally charge consumers whatever they want no matter what price decreases or trade promotions they receive from manufacturers. Coupons therefore have become one way for manufacturers to obtain more control over the prices consumers pay for their products.

Exhibit 4.2 A Coupon for a New Product

Source: Courtesy of Frito-Lay.

Coupon distribution has been much more prevalent in some categories than in others, and many consumers expect to be able to use a coupon each time they purchase one of these products. Categories where couponing is especially frequent include a variety of low-involvement, parity products (such as laundry products, household cleaners, ready-to-eat cereals, and coffee) that are subject to much consumer brand switching. It seems that manufacturers in these categories have often substituted price promotions for brand differentiation.

Although coupons are most often used for price discounts on inexpensive items, they have occasionally been used to promote high-value products. For example, Continental Airlines once ran a coupon in a variety of newspapers offering a round-trip ticket anywhere in the United States for $198, good only with the use of the coupon. High-value coupons may have serious problems with misredemption, however, so coupons for high-priced items are often used to call attention to a special promotion offered through the manufacturer (which may be valid only when the coupon is presented), rather than to give a certain amount off a set purchase price through a retailer.

Exhibit 4.3   A High-Value Coupon

Source: Courtesy of The Upjohn Company.

Problems with Coupon Usage

Despite the many advantages of coupons as a promotional tool, a number of problems are associated with their usage. As mentioned earlier, some companies have expressed interest in decreasing or even discontinuing their coupon distribution, for several reasons:

- Coupons tend to be an expensive and inefficient way of marketing products. Generally, less than 2 percent of the coupons distributed to consumers through free-standing inserts—the most popular type of distribution method—are redeemed. This means that the costs of such promotions per coupon redeemed can be quite high. For example, an FSI coupon with a cost of $7 per thousand and a 2 percent response rate would cost the manufacturer nearly 50 cents per coupon redeemed, including 35 cents in distribution costs and around 14 cents in retailer and clearinghouse fees. By reducing coupon usage, part of this expense may be passed on to consumers, some marketers argue.

- Although there is some disagreement about this in the academic literature, many marketers believe that excessive couponing erodes brand loyalty and encourages switching behaviors on the part of consumers.

- Coupons are frequently used by people who would have purchased the product at full price; this means that sales may not increase much despite the fact that per-item profitability has decreased.

- Like other sales promotions, couponing creates uneven demand for particular products throughout the year, complicating production and distribution issues for the manufacturer and making it more difficult for retailers to keep an appropriate amount of the product in stock.

Due to these factors, a number of companies have attempted to cut back on their use of coupons in recent years. Procter & Gamble, for instance, decreased its use of national couponing 50 percent from 1990 to 1996, and has even tested eliminating coupons entirely in certain markets. Nevertheless, certain problems are associated with this movement to decrease reliance on coupons. Studies show that at least some consumers seem to object strongly to manufacturers' attempts to reduce or eliminate the use of coupons: for example, during a test in upstate New York in 1995, more than 20,000 people signed a petition protesting Procter & Gamble's decision not to distribute coupons. (P & G and nine other firms later agreed to pay $4.2 million to consumers in that area in an anti-trust settlement since they had deprived them of the coupons.) In addition, since consumers in many categories are switchers and therefore more likely to purchase products when they have coupons for them, companies that decrease their use of coupons may find that their sales suffer dramatically, unless they have very strong brand loyalty or other companies follow suit.

Exhibit 4.4   A Cereal Company Ad to Reduce Couponing

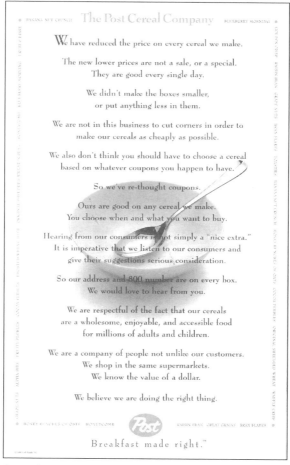

Source: Courtesy of Kraft General Foods.

Therefore, rather than attempting to eliminate coupons entirely, some manufacturers are trying to develop couponing programs designed to achieve specific marketing goals, instead of offering general discounts to the population as a whole. For instance, Kraft has developed a promotion to distribute coupons good for multiple purchases of its Miracle Whip salad dressing to people who are heavy users of the product, in the hope that if consumers have more product in their homes they will use even more of it. Post has distributed "universal" coupons good for any of its cereal brands to encourage variety seekers to stay with Post products and to prevent retailers from having to stock up on any one brand at a particular point in time. Many companies have started using direct mail or electronic distribution methods to target different kinds of coupons toward current versus competitive users, in order to decrease the likelihood that particularly large discounts will be passed on to people who would have purchased the product anyway.

Exhibit 4.5   A Universal Cereal Coupon

Source: Courtesy of Kraft General Foods.

Coupon Delivery

Coupons may be delivered to the consumer through a variety of channels. Some methods deliver coupons to a broad mass audience; others are targeted at specific consumers in order to achieve particular objectives.

Free-Standing Inserts (FSIS)

By far the most prevalent form of coupon delivery is through the free-standing insert (FSI). In the United States in 1995, about 83 percent of coupons were distributed through FSIS, which have grown enormously in popularity since the early 1980s.

FSIS generally consist of $8\frac{1}{2} \times 11$-inch "booklets" of four-color advertisements with coupons that are distributed in Sunday newspapers. Most FSIS are developed as cooperative ventures, with many noncompetitive marketers contributing materials and sharing the costs on a proportionate basis. FSIS are often coordinated by an outside firm, which charges marketers for printing and distribution to newspapers. Individual newspapers usually charge a flat fee per thousand to distribute the FSIS to consumers.

Exhibit 4.6   Consumers' Preferred Sources of Grocery and/or Health and Beauty Product Coupons*

Color Leaflets/Sunday Newspaper	64%
Receive in the Mail	59
Coupons/Weekly Newspaper Food Section	32
Inside/On the Product Package	31
From the Store Circular	26
At the Store	23
Magazines	15
Through Store Savings Clubs/Cards	15
At the Store Checkout After Purchase	9
Coupon Kiosk in Store	8
On the Street	2

*Of those using coupons in the past six months.

Source: Cox Couponing.

Exhibit 4.7   Coupon Distribution by Media Type (1995)

Fsi	83%
Newspaper	2
Direct Mail	3
Magazine	3
In-Pack	1
On-Pack	1
Instant On-Pack	1
Electronically Dispersed	1
Other	5

Source: NCH Promotional Services.

Exhibit 4.8   Redemption Rates by Media Type (1995)

	Grocery Products	Health and Beauty Products
Daily Newspaper ROP/Solo	0.7%	0.5%
Daily Newspaper Co-Op	0.4	0.2
Sunday Newspaper FSI	1.7	0.8
Sunday Supplement	1.0	—
Magazine On-Page	1.2	0.4
Magazine Pop-Up/Insert	1.0	1.4
Direct Mail	3.8	3.2
Regular In-Pack	8.8	5.4
Regular On-Pack	9.7	6.5
In-Pack Cross-Ruff	3.8	2.2
On-Pack Cross-Ruff	3.5	5.3
Instant On-Pack	31.3	33.5
Electronically Dispensed	8.0	7.4
On-Shelf Distributed	12.2	10.3
All Other Handout	4.6	3.3

Source: NCH Promotional Services.

Exhibit 4.9   An FSI with Attractive Graphics

Source: Courtesy of Ice Mountain Spring Water Company.

FSIS have a number of advantages. They provide a broad distribution at a relatively low price, $7 to $8 per thousand in 1996. Unlike advertisements printed inside the newspaper, FSIS may be targeted to a specific section of a metropolitan area. They also appear in color (generating consumer attention and discouraging forgery) and have room for a selling message and attractive graphics. In addition, FSIS are popular among consumers, partially because they appear in the same place in the paper each week and therefore are easy to find. Finally, because newspaper FSIS are distributed widely and are strong attention-getters, they can be effective in encouraging retailers to carry or stock up on a particular product.

Exhibit 4.10   An FSI with a Selling Message

Source: Courtesy of Kraft General Foods.

On the other hand, a number of disadvantages make FSIS inappropriate for many marketing programs with specific goals. Because they are distributed to a broad consumer base of newspaper readers, they tend to have a low redemption rate (an average of about 1.4 percent in 1995), and those who do redeem the coupons are frequently consumers who might have purchased the product even without the coupon. In addition, FSIS may not reach the intended target, due either to carelessness on the part of the newspaper's circulation department or to theft. Also, because some newspapers limit the number of insertions they accept each week, and because FSI "booklets" generally contain coupons only for non-competing products, it sometimes may be difficult for smaller companies to get FSIS placed. Finally, since insertions must be printed in advance and shipped to the newspapers, a long lead time is required.

Newspaper Run-of-Press (ROP)

About 1 percent of coupons are distributed run-of-press (ROP), meaning that they are printed inside the newspaper rather than inserted into it. The number of coupons distributed ROP has declined sharply during recent years as the number of FSIS has increased.

ROP coupons have a few advantages over free-standing inserts. They may be distributed on days other than Sunday, such as on a "best food day," and, since newspapers generally accept advertising up to a day or two before the run date, lead times are shorter. Also, newspapers are responsible for printing, and distribution is more certain with an ROP coupon than with an FSI (which may get lost before it reaches the consumer).

However, ROP ads usually do not allow the geographic targeting that is possible with FSIS, and they generally cannot be printed in four-color (so they may be overlooked by consumers or counterfeited). ROP advertising also tends to be expensive compared to FSIS. In addition, ROP coupons may be easily missed by consumers who don't read the entire paper, or who don't look closely at the ads. In general, ROP coupons tend to have even lower response rates than FSIS, with about 0.7 percent of the total number of coupons distributed typically being redeemed.

Direct Mail

About 3 percent of coupons are distributed to consumers through direct delivery, through either the U.S. Postal Service or an alter-

Exhibit 4.11 A Coupon Delivered Through Direct Mail

Source: Pepsi-Cola.

native delivery service. Direct-mail coupons may be mailed to consumers individually (usually with other selling materials about the product and possibly with a product sample). They may also be delivered as part of a group of coupons; a well-known example of this kind of delivery is the Carol Wright co-op mailing, which includes coupons from a variety of manufacturers.

Delivery of coupons by mail has several advantages. Perhaps the most important of these is selectivity: direct mail allows coupons to be targeted toward particular consumers based on where they live, their demographics, or their previous buying behaviors. Information about consumers may be obtained from a number of sources, such as public data of individual's age, gender, marital status, and other characteristics; responses from questionnaires conducted by firms such as Carol Wright; and a company's own databased information about consumers' responses to sweepstakes, rebates, and other promotions. Although individual direct mailings usually allow companies more selectivity, co-op mailings also allow some targeting to broad lifestyle groups such as young mothers, baby boomers, or retired people.

Exhibit 4.12   Carol Wright Co-Op Service Coupons

Source: Courtesy of Donnelley Marketing.

The selectivity of direct-mail couponing can allow marketers to achieve a number of goals. For instance, through the selection of a combination of different demographic or psychographic variables, consumers who are especially likely to be interested in a particular product, or who are apt to be users of a competitive product, can be specifically targeted. Knowledge of past behaviors can permit even more accurate targeting, so promotional goals can be more specific.

The selectivity of direct-mail couponing can be useful in a number of other ways. In contrast to FSIs and other mass-distribution methods of couponing, direct mail can help marketers ensure that only one coupon per household is used, reducing the likelihood that the promotion will cut into future profits. Perhaps because they are so targeted and because they are more infrequently received by consumers than are FSIs, direct-mail coupons tend to have relatively high redemption rates (an average of about 4 percent in 1995). Direct mail can also allow coupons to obtain broader distribution than FSIs, which are not received by households that do not purchase Sunday newspapers. This potentially broader coverage may be important to some manufacturers, particularly when companies are introducing new products or promoting brands that appeal to people who do not subscribe to major metropolitan newspapers, such as ethnic groups with many members who do not read English well.

Another advantage of direct mail is that it can act as a "secret weapon": since it may be difficult for competitors to find out how vigorously a coupon campaign is being conducted, it may be hard for them to counterattack. Finally, although FSIs tend to be cited as the most popular form of couponing, many consumers say they also appreciate receiving coupons through the mail, either individually or as part of co-op packages.

The major disadvantage of direct-mail couponing is its extremely high delivery cost, which can start at $15 or $20 per thousand for an untargeted mailing but may increase to many times this amount when specific types of individuals are targeted. This high cost includes purchasing mailing lists, printing the materials and envelopes, handling, and postage. Another disadvantage of direct mail is that it is often a poor trade motivator: while retailers are usually quite aware of which products are being promoted through FSIs or other mass-marketing couponing efforts, it may be difficult for sales representatives to persuade them that heavy direct mailings are indeed being conducted and will be successful at driving business for particular products in their stores.

Magazines

Magazines have decreased dramatically in popularity as a coupon delivery medium in recent years. Currently, only about 3 percent of coupons are delivered to consumers through magazines.

Magazine coupons may be of two types: on-page and "pop-up." On-page coupons are printed on the pages of the magazine; to use them, consumers must tear or cut out part of the page. Pop-up coupons are generally bound into the magazine next to an advertisement for the product, so that they pop up when the magazine is opened to that page. Pop-up coupons are more easily noticed and removed from the magazine, and generally they have redemption rates that are higher than in-page coupons. (This effectiveness is balanced by higher delivery costs, however.)

Delivery of coupons through magazines, though declining in popularity, has several advantages. Reproduction quality is high. Some magazines may also deliver a targeted audience appropriate to the particular product being promoted—for instance, disposable diapers may be couponed in *Parents* magazine.

Exhibit 4.13 Magazine Pop-Up Coupon

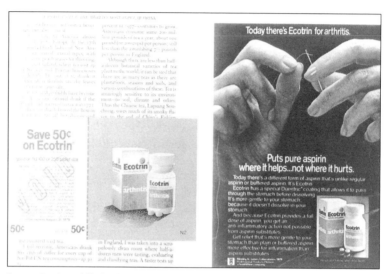

Source: Courtesy of Menley & James Laboratories.

The biggest problems in using magazines for coupon delivery are that most individual publications do not have very wide reach and that couponing in multiple magazines usually results in many consumers receiving duplicate coupons. In addition, although some publications offer regional editions, most magazines require coupons to be dropped on a nationwide basis, which is inappropriate for many marketing plans. The most targeted magazines also can be much more expensive than FSIs for a similar-sized ad and coupon, even though redemption rates tend to be somewhat lower than with FSIs (about 1 percent of coupons distributed through magazines were redeemed in 1995). Marketers also may find it difficult to use short redemption periods with some magazines, such as *National Geographic* or *The New Yorker*, since it may be quite some time before consumers get around to reading the whole publication and finding the coupons. Finally, many consumers do not like receiving coupons through magazines, perhaps because they cannot locate such coupons easily and do not appreciate having to cut holes in their magazines in order to use coupons.

Merchandise-Distributed Coupons

Coupons delivered to consumers in-pack or on-pack made up about 3 percent of all coupons delivered in the United States in 1995, a percentage that has declined during recent years.

In-pack coupons are included inside a package, often with a "flag" on the outside of the package calling attention to their presence. Special care must be taken with in-pack coupons, particularly if they are to be included in food products. There are quite stringent Food and Drug Administration restrictions on how and in what form the coupon may be placed in the box, and there may be certain paper and printing requirements as well. (In addition, in-pack coupons are simply inappropriate for certain kinds of products, such as soft drinks or liquid bleach.)

An alternative to the in-pack coupon is the on-pack coupon. On-pack coupons are attached to the package in some way or are printed as part of the package itself.

Coupons included in-pack or on-pack may apply to future purchases of the same product, future purchases of a different product, or (in some on-pack promotions) the current purchase of the product. Coupons for future purchases of the same product are generally designed to increase brand loyalty, particularly in a category where switching often occurs. For instance, Green Giant may include a coupon in its frozen spinach that can be used toward any Green Giant frozen vegetable, thereby increasing the likelihood that consumers will buy its products rather than a competitive brand in the future.

Coupons for other products—or "cross-ruffs"—are often used to create interest in less popular items made by the same manufacturer. For instance, Kraft might create awareness of a new packaged-rice side dish by placing a coupon for it in the company's popular Kraft American cheese singles. Cross-ruffs also are used when there is a connection between the product being purchased and the one being promoted. For instance, purchasers of nondairy creamer, who are assumed to be coffee drinkers, may be supplied with a coupon for a particular brand of coffee. In categories where variety is a component of purchase behavior, coupons for other brands in the same category may be used; for instance, Kellogg's may place coupons for a new cereal in boxes of Frosted Flakes. Coupons can be cross-ruffed in products made by other manufacturers, but in practice they are usually distributed in products made by the same manufacturer.

"Instant" coupons are attached to the outside of a product package, and can be removed by the consumer for an immediate discount on the price of the item currently being purchased. These coupons have an advantage over trade deals that also have the potential of offering instant savings because manufacturers can be sure the discount is passed on to the consumer. However, not all consumers notice instant coupons or bother to use them. Although the redemption rate of this kind of coupon is among the highest of all distribution types (32 percent in 1995), instant coupons are still redeemed by consumers less than a third of the time.

A major advantage of using in-pack and on-pack coupons is that they have practically no delivery cost, since a product that is already being distributed carries them. The "flag" on the front panel of the product can also provide a point of differentiation at the time of purchase, since some consumers may be more likely to buy a product if they can get a coupon. Since the manufacturer controls the distribution of the product, it is possible to restrict where the coupons are dropped. In addition, redemption rates of in-pack and on-pack coupons tend to be high.

One problem with in-pack or on-pack coupons is that they generally must have expiration dates that are well into the future or no expiration dates at all, because it is difficult to predict when the product that the coupon is being packaged with will be consumed. This allows consumers to use the coupons at their leisure. In addition, in-pack coupons may be overlooked by some consumers, and on-pack coupons sometimes may be difficult for them to remove. Finally, for on-pack coupons, special equipment or materials may be required to print the coupons on the package, increasing the packaging costs.

In summary, in-pack and on-pack coupons for future purchases of the same product attract no new users but they do reward existing customers who (depending on the circumstances) may buy the product again without a coupon. Therefore, they are most appropriate when the goal of a company is to increase brand loyalty—in categories where switching frequently occurs, for example. Coupons for other products also can be successfully delivered in-pack or on-pack, though care must be taken to ensure that the goods being promoted are an appropriate fit with the one being purchased. For example, Haagen-Dazs once included coupons touting the "Fat Free!" benefit of its sorbet in containers of its ultra-rich premium ice cream, a tactic that undoubtedly made many consumers feel particularly guilty about the product they currently were consuming. Similarly, Philip Morris probably would not want to include coupons for its discount brands in cartons of Marlboro, since this tactic might lead loyal users to trade down to products with lower profit margins.

Electronic Couponing

An increasingly popular method of coupon distribution is through the cash register. With the advent of point-of-purchase electronic scanners in most grocery store chains, several companies have created coupons good for future purchases that are distributed to consumers based on their current purchasing behaviors. For instance, a consumer who buys a can of Folger's coffee might receive a coupon for $1 off a can of Maxwell House coffee; the large discount is intended to be high enough to prompt a substitution in the future. In other cases, the purchase of a particular item may prompt the dispensing of coupons for related products. A consumer buying baby formula may receive a coupon for Huggies diapers or for a free photo sitting at a nearby Sears store.

Electronic couponing programs are usually developed by third-party companies that pay retailers to place the machines in their stores. Manufacturers of products then pay to have their brands couponed to consumers who meet certain purchasing criteria in particular stores over a period of time. The cost to manufacturers of placing coupons on the system usually depends on the type of promotion desired. For example, a manufacturer wanting to distribute coupons to competitors' customers should expect to pay more than one planning to target consumers buying complementary products, or to purchasers of the company's own brand.

An even more sophisticated type of electronic couponing is used by retailers offering card-based, frequent-shopper plans. Consumers enrolled in these plans present the retailer with a card that gives special discounts on items purchased on the current shopping trip. At some stores, swiping the card through an electronic reader allows the consumer's entire shopping history to be accessed by the computer. Coupons for future purchases can then be delivered, either immediately at the cash register or later through direct mail, based on the individual's purchases not only on the current shopping trip, but on all previous occasions when the card was used.

The use of electronic coupon delivery has a number of advantages. Most importantly, it allows companies to target coupons to consumers based on their current or previous purchasing habits, meaning that more specific promotional goals can be pursued. Electronic coupons generally have very high response rates (around 8 percent in 1995), due to their precise targeting and the generally high value of the discounts offered. While absolute costs of delivering coupons electronically are quite high (several cents each, depending on the type of customer being targeted), the high redemption rate means that the net cost for each redeemed coupon is comparable to that of FSIs. Electronic coupons also have shorter lead times than FSIs, allowing marketers to be more responsive in their promotional programs. Finally, since electronic coupons often are good only at the retail chain that distributed them, they tend to promote store loyalty and therefore are often favored by retailers.

These advantages have caused electronic coupons to grow quickly in popularity, with most major manufacturers in 1995 reporting that they had used them in recent months. Nevertheless, there are disadvantages associated with electronic couponing programs that tend to make them inappropriate as a company's only coupon-distribution method. For one thing, not all retailers participate in such programs, so sole reliance upon them will not ensure full coverage of a particular market. Despite the fact that redemption rates of electronic coupons are high, many consumers profess to dislike them, perhaps because receiving discounts for future purchases of other products at the checkout makes them feel frustrated that they have to wait until the next shopping trip to get the discount. Also, unlike FSIS, electronic coupons usually do not carry a selling message. This means they are most useful when they are accompanied by advertising campaigns through other channels, or when consumers have tried all the brands in a category and are at least somewhat inclined to switch, or when the category is perceived as a parity product (with little difference perceived to exist between brands).

Other Retailer-Based Coupons

Other methods of distributing coupons are also available at the point of purchase at many retail stores. For instance, some stores feature coupon dispensers near the product as it sits on the shelf; consumers merely have to remove a coupon and take it to the checkout in order to obtain their discount. Coupons are also available at some stores in centrally located kiosks. Finally, many retailers offer coupons to consumers in store circulars or advertisements that may be picked up in the store; manufacturers sometimes pay part of the costs associated with this type of promotion.

In the past, on-shelf coupons were usually placed by distribution representatives who stocked the product in the store. In recent years, however, most major retailers willing to use on-shelf coupons have made arrangements with third-party vendors who place dispensers (some of them electronic) next to the products of marketers who have paid for the service. Retailers prefer the setup because it ensures a cleaner and more uniform look for their stores. Also, some manufacturers appreciate the assurance that their plans to have coupons available at the point of purchase are more likely to be implemented when a specialty company assumes that responsibility.

Coupons located next to the product on the shelf have the primary advantage of drawing attention to a particular brand at the place where consumers make their final purchasing decisions. This may be especially useful in categories where products without a great deal of differentiation compete for consumer attention—for example, pain relievers or spaghetti sauce. This type of couponing program also may be targeted very narrowly, at the store or regional level, allowing manufacturers to implement micro-marketing plans.

On the other hand, on-shelf coupons may be used by many consumers who were planning to buy the product anyway (including some who would have missed an FSI), so this method may be less than appropriate for products that already dominate a category. (Because shelf dispensers are so prominent, coupons distributed in this manner generally have higher redemption rates than even "instant on-pack" coupons; nevertheless, almost half of the consumers purchasing such products forget to use them, or choose not to, when they pay for their purchases.) In addition, since generally only one product, or a few brands in a category are couponed at once, many companies in crowded categories may be unable to use this type of promotion or may have to wait a long time to be able to offer discounts.

Coupons are also offered at centrally located kiosks in some stores. The more traditional kiosks offer rows of paper coupons to consumers, while electronic kiosks enable consumers to request coupons by looking through an on-screen menu that tells them what discounts are available. While kiosks have the advantage of offering discounts to consumers at the point of purchase, they have a number of disadvantages that make them inappropriate for many marketing programs. For one thing, many consumers feel rushed when they visit stores and do not want to take the time to search for coupons. People who do look for bargains at a kiosk may be extremely price-sensitive consumers who will demonstrate no long-term loyalty no matter how well the product performs. In addition, the more traditional kiosks often run out of paper coupons quickly, while electronic kiosks tend to attract bored youngsters who are relatively unlikely to purchase the products being couponed. Therefore, kiosk promotions tend to be most useful for companies that want to achieve a short-term sales gain—even at a lower profit margin—and have no expectations of achieving related sales in the future.

A final type of retailer-oriented couponing tactic is through the store's advertisements or promotional circulars. Many retailers attempt to attract consumers simply by lowering the price of products to everyone who makes a purchase during a certain period of time (a practice that will be discussed in the chapter on trade deals), but some require consumers to present a coupon in order to get the discount. Circulars are often available in the store, however, for people who did not bring a coupon with them. In some circumstances, retailers pay the cost of promotions advertised in circulars; in others, however, manufacturers shoulder some or all of the costs. An advantage of this kind of coupon program over the use of FSIs is that retailers tend to support their own promotions heavily: for example, they are more likely to make certain that enough product is on hand to meet demand and may display the brand prominently in the store. A comparative disadvantage, on the other hand, is that these types of promotions do little to change attitudes about the product, since the coupons offered by retailers are generally printed in one or two colors on newsprint and include only the brand name and the price.

Finally, coupons may be distributed to consumers in conjunction with sampling programs inside the store. This method of couponing often works quite well, since it encourages consumers to make a purchase when they are actively considering the merits of the product.

Other Coupon Distribution Methods

A relatively new coupon-distribution method used occasionally by a few companies is to send coupons only to consumers who ask for them. Such requests generally are made through the use of a toll-free telephone number or on-line interactive marketing site communicated by a company's general advertising or public-relations efforts. The disadvantages of this kind of promotion are obvious: many consumers may not bother to call a company simply to request a coupon, and others may lose interest in the product by the time the coupon arrives in their mailbox. However, couponing by request does give a company the names and addresses of prospective users, and this information can be put to good use later through database marketing efforts. In addition, request-only promotions can help companies make sure that each consumer receives only one coupon for a particular product, a feature that can be especially advantageous when very large discounts are being offered.

Exhibit 4.14   Coupon Distributed By Request

Source: Courtesy of Rubbermaid, Inc., and Procter & Gamble.

In another type of distribution, coupons are handed to consumers directly, either on the street or in other public places such as movie theaters or shopping centers. This method is often considered to be relatively expensive and also may be annoying to consumers who are preoccupied with other matters. However, when used in conjunction with sampling, this type of couponing can be helpful in introducing consumers to new products. SmartFood, for example, enjoyed an extremely successful launch of its cheese-flavored popcorn snack primarily through the use of this tactic in trend-setting metropolitan markets.

Finally, some creative companies have attempted to develop ways to deliver coupons wherever individuals have access to them. For example, a controversial program placed coupons for goods and services on luncheon menus sent home to parents of California schoolchildren. Other programs have distributed coupons in such non-traditional channels as health clubs, meals served by airlines, or even restrooms. Such experiments probably should be expected to continue as advertising and promotional clutter in the marketplace becomes more prevalent and companies find it increasingly difficult to capture consumers' attention.

Issues in Couponing
Value

Using coupons has saved consumers an increasingly large amount of money in recent years. The average face value of redeemed coupons in 1995 was 68 cents, compared to only 35 cents in 1985. The increasingly large values of coupons offered by marketers has been fueled by scanner data suggesting that low-value coupons tend to be redeemed by a brand's current users: to get competitive users to switch brands, a larger-value coupon often must be offered. Some manufacturers have also started to offer larger-value coupons to maintain good relations with store chains offering double- or triple-couponing promotions, since coupons over a certain value (for example, those in excess of 50 cents) are usually not eligible for the additional discount paid for by retailers.

Most consumers appear to have a threshold of value under which they will not use a coupon for a particular product. However, most studies show that increasing the value of a coupon beyond that threshold does not greatly increase the likelihood that consumers will use a coupon. Therefore, marketers should probably try to identify the types of consumers they want to influence and set coupon values near those consumers' thresholds for their products.

Consumers seem to have different expectations about the value of coupons for different categories of products. This attitude appears to be unrelated to the retail price of the products, and is instead probably determined by the typical discounts offered in each category. Discounts on pet products tend to be higher than those on frozen entrees, for example.

A primary reason that most coupons today are of relatively high value is that many manufacturers use them as tools to introduce users of competitive products to the brand. Although the number of consumers who switch only if a coupon is of high value may be few, those people are much less likely to be regular users of the product, and getting them to become triers may result in long-term value. Using high-value coupons may be a conscious decision of marketers to sacrifice profits on a single coupon drop in exchange for increased trial and brand loyalty.

Exhibit 4.15 Average Face Value of Redeemed Coupons

1985	35 cents		1991	54 cents
1986	38		1992	58
1987	40		1993	60
1988	44		1994	63
1989	47		1995	68
1990	50			

Source: NCH Promotional Services.

Exhibit 4.16 Top 20 Products in Coupon Distribution (1995)

1. Cereals and Breakfast Foods
2. Medications, Remedies, and Health Aids
3. Household Cleaners
4. Pet Food
5. Hair Care
6. Oral Hygiene
7. Packaged Meats
8. Detergents
9. Condiments, Gravies, Sauces
10. Bread and Baked Goods
11. Skin Care Preparations
12. Personal Soap and Bath Additives
13. Cough and Cold Remedies
14. Prepared Foods
15. Paper Products
16. Ice Cream Novelties
17. Household Supplies
18. Fresheners, Deodorizers
19. Vitamins
20. Deodorant

Source: NCH Promotional Services.

The Message

While coupons may be of any size or shape, advertisers usually try to make them the shape of a dollar bill. This makes them easier

Exhibit 4.17   A Coupon "Game" Circular

Source: Courtesy of Sears, Roebuck and Co.

for the consumer, the retailer, and the clearinghouse to handle. While there are no specific physical requirements for coupons, the cardinal rule is: *If it is a coupon, make it look like a coupon.*

An important part of the coupon is what is called the "boiler-plate," or details of the offer. This is simply the copy that explains the coupon to both the consumer and the retailer. This information may appear on the front or (sometimes) the back of the coupon.

Coupons should make the offer boldly and clearly, expressly stating the limitations. It is also worth noting that placing too many restrictions on usage (such as requiring that only certain products in a line or certain sizes are eligible) may not produce the antici-pated results, because the retailer (who has no incentive to make sure that the coupon is redeemed properly) may allow consumers to use a coupon even if the exact product specified isn't purchased or even stocked in the store. Therefore keeping the offer simple may help to ensure that the anticipated success will be achieved.

One new type of promotion attempts to turn coupon usage into a "game" by covering the printed value of the discount with a material to be rubbed off or otherwise removed, either at home or in the retail store. Although this type of coupon is new and hasn't been tested much, it appears that many consumers may be willing to uncover the amount to determine how much they have "won." It is less likely that consumers will visit a store to determine the value of their coupons, and some customers may even be annoyed by this type of promotion.

Coupon Redemption

One of the great uncertainties of sales promotion is the rate at which product coupons will be redeemed. Although averages for different kinds of delivery methods have been determined, redemptions rates can also depend on specific factors affecting the category, brand, and consumer.

For instance, products that are used by only a small percentage of the population (such as denture cream) will obviously have a smaller redemption rate than products that are used by almost everyone (such as laundry detergent), all else being equal. Placing restrictions on product size can decrease redemption, as may offering a low face value or small percentage of the total purchase price. (For instance, offering a $5 discount on a new car is not likely to excite many consumers.) The amount of brand loyalty in the category and the degree (and appropriateness) of the selection of the delivery process can also be important factors, as can the area of the country in which the coupon is delivered. Retail distribution of the product is also a big factor, since consumers may throw away coupons for brands they can't find in the store. The share of the market of a particular product, the competitive activity in the category, and the degree of product familarity also may have some effect on redemption rates, although these factors appear to be less important.

Misredemption

Misredemption of coupons can be a serious problem, particularly for companies that distribute high-value coupons. Coupon misredemption may sometimes occur because of carelessness on the

Exhibit 4.18   Number of Coupons Redeemed

1985	6.5 billion	1991	7.5 billion
1986	7.1	1992	7.7
1987	7.2	1993	6.8
1988	7.1	1994	6.2
1989	7.1	1995	5.8
1990	7.1		

Source: NCH Promotional Services.

part of the retailer; in other cases it may be much more deliberate and methodical.

Since retailers are being reimbursed for the full amount of the coupon, they often are not as careful about redeeming them as they might be if the money were coming out of their own pockets. For example, a harried grocery store clerk who is presented with 20 coupons and $150 worth of groceries is unlikely to check to make certain that all the coupons are for items actually being purchased, since doing so would slow down the line and annoy customers. In addition, retailers and consumers may be lax about checking that the correct size or variety of an item is purchased or that the coupon has not expired.

A second way that coupons may be misredeemed is through organized "gang punching." Gang punchers steal or otherwise obtain great quantities of FSIs and punch out the coupons. Those coupons are then redeemed through unscrupulous retailers or through phony store addresses. (In a few cases, too, dishonest retailers may pay consumers who don't use the coupon a percentage of its face value, then redeem it for the full amount from the manufacturer.)

Although laxness on the part of retailers can be a problem for manufacturers, most companies have devoted a relatively small amount of resources to confronting the issue. Because these misredemptions tend to be scattered among many retailers, they are hard to spot; in addition, making too much of this issue may jeopardize marketers' relationships with legitimate and important retailers. To some extent, the problem is beginning to resolve itself, as some larger retailers have begun to scan coupons at the checkout counter; if the coupon does not match a purchase or has expired, then it is not accepted. Marketers who are concerned about consumer misredemptions through legitimate retailers should include bar codes on their coupons, and they might consider offering some kind of incentive to retailers who scan them.

Some manufacturers have clamped down much harder on organized coupon misredemptions. Marketers are on the lookout for coupons that appear to be too neatly and uniformly cut out; for stores that have a higher-than-expected volume of coupon redemptions; and for new retailers at unverified addresses. Nevertheless, organized misredemptions remain a problem for coupon issuers.

The following points may be helpful for marketers who hope to minimize misredemptions:

- Make coupons difficult to duplicate or counterfeit, perhaps by the use of four-color printing or a special kind of paper.

- Treat coupons as money.

- Make certain that expiration dates are easy to find and read.

- Avoid using excessive values in coupons; keep them within reason.

- Avoid using values that exceed the cost of the media in which the coupons are distributed or that exceed the value of the product.

- Keep the offer clear and uncomplicated, making it easy for consumers and retailers to understand.

- Set a redemption policy and stick to it; don't hesitate to refuse payment for redemptions that are clearly fraudulent.

- Match coupon redemptions with store sales to spot stores with unusually high redemption rates.

Multiple-Purchase Coupons

Multiple-purchase coupons require consumers to buy more than one product in order to get a discount. About 13 percent of all coupons distributed in 1995 were of this type. Multiple-purchase coupons include offers allowing consumers to get a free product when a purchase is made as well as discounts on multiple units of the same product. As might be expected, redemption rates for most multiple-purchase coupons are considerably lower than those

Exhibit 4.19   A Multiple-Product Coupon

Source: Courtesy of Procter & Gamble.

of single-purchase coupons. Nevertheless, a majority of coupon users report having used a multiple-purchase coupon; as expected, heavy coupon users are especially likely to have done so.

Multiple-purchase coupons may be especially useful in getting people who are already loyal to a particular product to consume even more of it. For example, Kraft found through research studies that the best targets for additional usage of Miracle Whip were people who already purchased the product on a regular basis. The company therefore began offering coupons for multiple containers of the product, accompanied by recipes that suggested new uses. The promotion therefore ensured that heavy users would have enough product on hand to try the recipes while decreasing the likelihood that consumers would use the coupons for products they would have purchased anyway. Similar usages of multiple-product coupons also may be appropriate for other categories such

Exhibit 4.20 A Multiple-Product Coupon: Buy Two, Get One Free

Source: Courtesy of First Brands.

as soft drinks, cookies, or other snack foods, where individuals are likely to consume more of the product if they have it on hand.

Costs

There are two types of costs connected with coupons: those involved with distribution and those involved with redemption. Distribution costs are incurred in getting the coupons to the consumer, such as printing, placing the print ad or FSI, and postage for direct mail. Redemption costs are associated with the payment and allocation of the discount to the consumer, the retailer, and any middlemen.

Determining distribution costs is straightforward and can easily be done in advance of the execution of the program. Most companies or publications offering coupon distribution quote on a cost per thousand basis, making media relatively easy to compare. Marketers must only be certain that everything (such as printing costs, list rental, or postage) is included.

Redemption costs are more tricky, since they require marketers to estimate how many people will actually redeem the coupon. Because that cannot always be predicted accurately (especially for new products or for those in categories where competitive activities have changed), predicting this portion of couponing costs can sometimes be difficult. Nevertheless, an anticipated redemption rate range can usually be predicted with considerable accuracy.

Redemption costs usually consist of the face value of the coupon plus the various costs of the redemption process. Normally, in addition to the discount given to consumers, retailers are allowed a set price per redeemed coupon to cover handling costs. Handling costs paid to retailers in 1996 were 8 cents per coupon.

Because of the large volume of coupons redeemed by the 30,000 or so mass retailers in the United States, manufacturers do not deal individually with each retailer. Instead, manufacturers and retailers both use clearinghouses, which act in a similar fashion to banks in making payments and clearing documents. Retailers generally forward their coupons to a retailer clearinghouse, which pays them the face value of the coupon and the handling charge. The retail clearinghouse then forwards the coupons to the clearinghouse hired by the manufacturer. The manufacturer clearinghouse checks the coupons for their validity and reimburses the retail clearinghouse. The manufacturer pays fees of between $6.25 to $13 per thousand to the retail clearinghouse and $45 to $50 per thousand to the manufacturer clearinghouse.

As an example, a coupon for 50 cents may generate 100,000 redemptions, half of which were incremental volume (meaning that the product wouldn't have been sold without the coupon). Total redemption costs would be $63,200 (50 cents face value + 8 cents retailer handling fee times 100,000 redemptions plus $700 for retail clearinghouse fees plus $4,500 for manufacturer clearinghouse fees). A typical distribution cost for this type of response might be $35,000, bringing the total cost of the promotion to $98,200.

Typically, these distribution and redemption costs are compared with the incremental profits generated by the increased volume from the coupon. In this example, assume that the manufacturer's profit on each item sold is 75 cents. This amount is then multiplied by the incremental volume generated by the coupon (in this instance, 75 cents $\times$ 50,000 = $37,500). This total

Exhibit 4.21   Average Expiration Periods

1988	5.9 months	1992	4.0 months
1989	5.3	1993	3.1
1990	4.9	1994	3.4
1991	4.1	1995	3.3

Source: NCH **Promotional Services.**

can be compared to the cost of the promotion to judge whether it provided immediate additional profits.

However, this type of profit analysis leaves out the important issue of the residual value of coupon promotions. Often, coupon programs are designed to generate consumer trial at the expense of an immediate loss in profits, in the hope that some of the triers will purchase the product at full price in the future. In addition, many coupon delivery systems such as FSIs or direct mail also have a secondary advertising function, in that they can point out product benefits or remind consumers to purchase the brand. Therefore, even though some coupon promotions may appear at first to be unprofitable, they actually may be very valuable to the brand over the long run.

Expiration Dates

The trend in couponing is toward significantly shorter redemption periods. For example, the average redemption period dropped to 3 months in 1996 from 5.9 months in 1985 and 10 months in 1980, according to NCH Promotional Services. In contrast, only about 1 percent of coupons distributed in 1996 had no expiration date, compared to more than 23 percent in 1985.

There are several reasons for this trend toward shorter redemption periods. For one thing, limiting the time span for a coupon's redemption can help marketing managers plan more effectively, and it may allow them to better judge the results of their promotional activities. Shorter redemption periods also help limit a company's financial liabilities, which may be important for accounting reasons. In addition, the presence of an expiration date may produce a temporary increase in sales, since many consumers may rush to use the coupon while it is still good.

Most important, however, is that shorter redemption periods can affect the profile of the consumer using the coupon. Often, consumers who stockpile coupons and use them long after they have been distributed are people who either use the product regularly already, or are very promotion sensitive and buy only on deal. Limiting the amount of time during which coupons can be redeemed appears to make it more likely that people who redeem the coupons will be those who do not already buy the product, and who may continue to purchase it in the future even without the coupon.

The trend toward shorter redemption periods is not without its drawbacks, however. For example, research has shown that people who use coupons relatively infrequently often complain that they do not have enough time to use coupons with short redemption periods before they expire. Since light coupon users may be less price-sensitive than people who use coupons more often, it is possible that marketers who offer coupons with very short redemption periods may be missing out on the opportunity to convert people who might demonstrate long-term loyalty to their products. In addition, some situations demand longer redemption periods. For example, in-pack and on-pack coupons may not be found or used by consumers for a long time; therefore expiration dates should usually be at least a year or two after the product is distributed. Coupons for infrequently purchased products sometimes may have longer redemption periods to give the consumer more time to replenish the product.

The Strategic Use of Coupons

Used properly, coupons can be an effective way to achieve a variety of strategic objectives with many different kinds of consumers.

Loyal Users

Coupons can be very effective at reinforcing sales to loyal users. Coupons targeted at current users of a product may be placed in-pack or on-pack; consumers who are coupon-sensitive may also use coupons distributed through other channels. Whether these consumers would have purchased the product without the coupon, however, is less clear-cut.

Coupons may, in some cases, encourage loyal users to purchase and consume a larger quantity of a product. For instance, a consumer who would ordinarily buy a small package of Oreo cookies might be persuaded to buy a larger package or two packages if a coupon is good only on the larger size or on multiple units. As mentioned earlier, this strategy may be particularly effective if loyal consumers are likely to consume more of the product once they have it in their homes, since this means that the promotion will be less apt to cannibalize future sales.

Current customers of a product may be persuaded to purchase other additional products through the use of cross-ruff in-pack or on-pack coupons. This generally works best when the two products are somehow related to one another, or when the purchase of one product indicates that another product may also be needed. For instance, a diaper package may appropriately include a coupon for baby wipes.

Coupons targeted directly at current users of a product (for instance, through on-packs, electronically at the cash register, or as a result of databased information about individuals) are often of low value or for multiple units. The logic is that these people are unlikely to need a large incentive to be persuaded to buy the brand again, and that additional discounts given to these individuals should be viewed as lost profits. A contrasting view, however, is that in order to ensure continued brand loyalty, current users of a product should receive particularly good treatment, including the lowest prices currently available in the marketplace. This "relationship marketing" approach may be especially important in more competitive product categories, since even consumers who like a particular brand may defect if they constantly receive high-value coupons or discounts on other products but must pay close to the full price on the one they currently use.

Competitive Loyals

Consumers who are intensely loyal to a particular product are unlikely to be influenced by a coupon for another brand, but people who are only moderately brand-loyal may be influenced by coupons. In a survey conducted by Manufacturers Coupon Control Center, more than 75 percent of consumers who were loyal to a particular product stated that they might be willing to purchase another brand if they received a coupon for it. However, many of these people may switch only if the coupon is of high value. Since companies cannot afford to give high discounts to all their customers, specific targeting methods such as electronic couponing or direct marketing may be useful at targeting these high-value coupons to people who are—or seem likely to be—competitive users.

Many consumers who use a high-value coupon to purchase a product other than the one they usually buy may go back to their former brand the next time they make a purchase, but some may continue to purchase the couponed product into the future. This may be especially true if the brand being promoted has some real benefit over the other product that can be fully communicated only through product usage, and if the product has not been used in the past, as is the case with new products. In addition, a high-value coupon may lead some people to break habitual patterns and thus be more likely to use other brands in the future.

Switchers

Consumers who buy a variety of brands tend to be excellent prospects for coupons. The fact that the percentage of consumers identified as switchers has increased during recent years may, in fact, partially account for the rising usage of coupons by manufacturers.

Consumers who switch from one brand to another depending on which seems to be the best value at the time are very likely to be influenced by coupons, provided that they are coupon users. People who have used a particular brand before may be persuaded to buy it again with a price incentive. And people who have never tried a particular brand, but who are not especially loyal to any one competitive brand, may use a coupon on a new brand, provided that the redemption value is sufficiently high. Insofar as coupons induce consumers to try new brands they may ultimately add to long-term brand value by increasing the likelihood that those people may buy the brand in the future.

Consumers who are variety seekers may also be strongly affected by coupons, which may give them an extra incentive to buy a specific brand. Coupons are not likely to increase long-term brand value very much with variety seekers, however, since these consumers benefit by using a variety of different products. Marketers of brands in categories where variety is a benefit tend to cross-ruff when using in-pack and on-pack coupons; for instance, General Mills may place a coupon for its Crispy Wheats 'n' Raisins in boxes of Wheaties.

Coupons may also be of some help in gaining or maintaining distribution for new or low-selling brands. Coupons may increase demand for certain brands at the retail level; in addition, retailers may fear that if consumers fail to find a couponed brand in the store, they may shop at another store for it.

Price Buyers

Consumers who look only at price when making purchasing decisions may be persuaded to buy through the use of coupon promotions if the value of the coupon is high enough to bring the price of the product below that of its competitors. However, without a similar discount in the future, these consumers are likely to go back to purchasing whatever brand costs least.

Nonusers

Coupons generally do very little to persuade nonusers in a particular category to make a purchase. The rare exception may be when consumers are persuaded by a high-value coupon to purchase a brand; in that case, if they like the brand and use it again in the future, long-term value may have been created. This probably occurs very rarely, however.

The Residual Value of Coupons

Coupons can often be successful at creating long-term value for a brand. They may persuade people who do not currently use a particular brand to try it; if these consumers like it, they may purchase it again in the future. In addition, couponing may help brands to obtain or maintain distribution, which can also result in long-term sales increases.

While some forms of distribution such as direct-mail and electronic couponing have the potential of targeting coupons to consumers based on their previous buying behaviors, this information is difficult to obtain for many product categories. Until such data are more easily accessible, therefore, most mass marketers will probably need to accept the fact that the coupon promotions they conduct will include some inefficiencies.

The difficult part of creating residual value with coupons, however, is in reaching the right consumers with the right offer. The most commonly cited problem in couponing is that discounts large enough to convince competitive users to try the brand are likely to be used to an even greater extent by loyals who very well might have purchased the brand anyway.

Because of this issue, marketers must make very clear decisions in advance about the goals they want to achieve with their couponing programs. Marketers who are using high-value coupons to prompt trial by new users generally need to resign themselves to sacrificing profits (or, at best, breaking even), due to redemptions by current customers who would have purchased the brand anyway. On the other hand, marketers may generate a sales spike and make a profit by distributing a coupon with a relatively low value, but this should not be assumed to create many new customers or add much long-term value.

CHAPTER FIVE

Special Packs

Bonus packs, in-packs, on-packs, near-packs, and specialty containers are all similar in that they give the consumer something extra at the point of purchase. As such, they can be useful at driving impulse purchases, thereby increasing sales. In addition, some of these promotions may be successful at increasing the long-term value of brands in certain situations.

Types of Special Packs

Bonus Packs

The bonus pack normally consists of a special container, package, carton, or other holder in which the consumer is given more of the product than usual for the same price or perhaps even a lower price. The idea of the bonus pack is similar to that of the "baker's dozen," in which 13 items (such as doughnuts) are sold for the price of 12.

Exhibit 5.1   Bonus Pack: Larger Container

Source: Courtesy H. J. Heinz Company.

Exhibit 5.2   Bonus Pack: Extra Unit

Source: Courtesy of Armour-Dial, Inc.

Bonus packs are often used with products that are fairly low in cost, that have high velocity (that is, are used up quickly), and in which additional product is a desirable reward in the eyes of the consumer. In addition, more successful bonus pack programs may succeed in advertising the extra product as an especially good value, or in tying it to a special promotion. For example, McDonald's once ran a tie-in with the dinosaur movie *Jurassic Park* in which it offered triple cheeseburgers, extra-large fries, and 32-ounce soft drinks.

Bonus packs are often used as an attempt to either reward or retain present customers and to take them out of the market for a longer period of time after the purchase—a ploy that is likely to be especially effective when competitors are expected to be promoting. Bonus packs can also be a successful method of getting attention at the point of purchase for parity products, as well as a sound way of presenting a price reduction to consumers.

The downside of bonus packs is that they can be expensive to implement. Although the cost of the additional product is often small, the new packaging and special handling required may be quite expensive. Retailers may also dislike bonus packs, especially if they are too large to fit in the space regularly allotted to the product in the store or warehouse; in some cases retailers may even refuse to carry them.

Bonus packs are generally unappealing to consumers who don't usually buy the product (the feeling is "If I don't usually use Brand X, why would I want two instead of one?"), and they do little to enhance brand value. Consumers may, in many cases, not believe that they are really getting extra product for their money, suspecting instead that the product is actually being sold at regular price.

In addition, manufacturers should be aware that bonus packs held together with a paper or rubber band can be taken apart, with the extra product either stolen by members of the distribution channel or sold separately. It therefore may be wise to make it difficult to remove the extra product (for instance, by gluing the packages together or by encasing them in plastic rather than just using a band, or by labeling each item with a notation that it is part of a larger package and is not to be sold separately).

In-Packs and On-Packs

Both in-packs and on-packs give consumers some sort of immediate reward (other than extra product or a price discount) for purchasing a brand. The product is often an item that is likely to be attractive to the targeted consumer, or it may be another product for the consumer to sample.

Exhibit 5.3   In-Pack Premium

Source: Cracker Jack® is the trademark of Borden, Inc., for candied popcorn and peanuts.

In-pack premiums are placed inside the package and range from the "Toy Surprise" found inside boxes of Cracker Jack popcorn to the towels, sheets, or dishes once found inside detergent boxes. This type of premium, for example, is often used in the children's segment of the ready-to-eat breakfast cereal category, since the promise of a small toy is generally attractive to youngsters.

Exhibit 5.4   In-Pack Premium: Cap'n Crunch Cereal

Source: Courtesy of Quaker Oats Company.

Exhibit 5.5   An On-Pack Premium of a Related Product

Source: Courtesy of The Gillette Company.

Exhibit 5.6   An On-Pack Premium

Source: Courtesy of 3M.

An on-pack premium is attached to the product or product package in some way. For example, it might be attached to the product with a paper or rubber band, or blister-packed inside plastic. Often the product and the on-pack premium are related—shaving creams with razors, canned cat foods with plastic can covers, or spices with recipe books. Premiums may also consist of other products sold by the same manufacturer or by other companies, since on-packs can provide a sampling vehicle for new or less-popular products.

Although in-packs and on-packs are usually sold at the regular price of the product, there may be situations where a particularly attractive premium will allow the price to be raised to cover some of the additional cost.

In-packs and on-packs may differentiate the product at the point of sale and may be used to appeal to specific segments of the population. In addition, certain premiums may increase usage by reminding the consumer of the brand. For example, recipe books may encourage use of specialty foods such as cardamom or other spices; soup bowls may provide reminders for a particular brand of soup; and coffee mugs may increase coffee consumption.

In-pack and on-pack promotions may also be attractive to some marketers in that the cost of the promotion may be determined in advance. Because the manufacturer can decide how many special packages will be produced and shipped, that number may be increased or decreased to conform to budgetary constraints.

In-packs and on-packs have many of the same negatives as bonus packs, however. They can be expensive to manufacture and distribute, and they may be refused by retailers if they don't fit in assigned spaces on store shelves or in the warehouse. Pretesting can be expensive, since it involves setting up the production lines to create the special products. If the premium is very attractive and is not securely packaged, theft or pilferage by consumers or store personnel may be a problem. Finally, some consumers who don't want the premium may decide not to buy the product at all, especially if the premium increases the price of the product.

Marketers who place in-packs inside food items should be aware of FDA regulations covering the types of materials that may be used, as well as how consumers will respond to finding these items inside their food purchases. For example, Coca-Cola once ran a sweepstakes where dollar bills—along with saline solution—were placed inside random cans of Coke. The company received substantial negative publicity, however, when some consumers drank the saline solution in the "MagicCans" and complained to the media about the taste. The failure of this promotion shows how important it is to consider consumer reaction to in-pack programs, even when they are legally acceptable.

Near-Packs

The near-pack is offered free, or for an additional charge, with the product at the point of purchase. (When there is an extra charge involved, it may be called a *salable* or *price-plus pack*.)

Near-packs may be used because a premium is too large or too inconvenient to be attached to the regular product; the bulkiness of the premium may therefore lend itself to a display. For example, Lever Brothers, working with the Marvel Comic Group, once developed a special near-pack Spiderman comic book to be given away with Aim toothpaste. The comic book focused on proper dental care as a storyline, and it was displayed in the toothpaste section of retail stores.

Near-packs have often been used at the retail level to generate store traffic. For instance, Burger King may give away drinking glasses to consumers purchasing certain menu items; Dunkin' Donuts may give away a free doughnut with a coupon when a coffee is purchased; gas stations may give away bottles of Coca-Cola or hats promoting NFL teams to drivers filling up their gas tanks; and supermarkets may give away dishes or encyclopedia volumes to consumers buying a certain dollar amount of groceries.

Exhibit 5.7   A Near-Pack Offer

Source: Courtesy of Dunkin' Donuts.

Like in-packs and on-packs, near-packs may be successful at generating interest in a dull product category. In addition, if the items are part of a series (for example, "Collect all six 'Star Wars' figures"), they can generate repeat purchases as consumers strive to obtain the whole set. Near-packs are very flexible, and they may get displays for packaged goods into retail outlets that choose to accept them. Near-packs may also be useful in generating trial for other items in a product line—for instance, many cosmetic companies offer "bonus days" where purchasers of one item at the regular price can receive a special collection of lipsticks, moisturizers, perfumes, or other items either free or at a low price.

Like other special packs, near-packs can also be used as a sampling device for products likely to appeal to consumers purchasing the brand being promoted. For example, Mattel found that its sales of toy cars and building blocks increased after McDonald's included the products as premiums with its Happy Meals.

However, many retailers dislike near-packs (except for the ones that they themselves use to lure consumers into the store), as they believe that they can be a lot of trouble to stock, handle, display, and monitor. Near-packs may also sometimes compete with other products that the retailer sells (for instance, a lawnmower manufacturer that gives away hedge clippers with purchases may find that many of its retailers also sell hedge clippers), which could result in lower overall retail profits for the retailer if consumers don't have to buy the items being offered as premiums. Therefore manufacturers may not be able to get as many stores to agree to carry near-packs as they might like.

In addition, manufacturers that use near-packs also face the possibility that retailers may not display them properly or that the premiums may be stolen by retail employees or by consumers. For these reasons, near-packs are often restricted to situations where the marketer of the product has control over the handling of the premiums, such as when the manufacturer operates or controls retail stores (as is the case with fast-food outlets and gas stations) or when distribution can be controlled by marketer-employed personnel (such as at department store cosmetic counters).

Specialty Containers

A specialty container often provides the consumer with a premium that can be used after the product it holds is consumed. Some examples of these kinds of reusable containers include the jelly jar glasses that once graced many homes in the United States, or tomato juice packed in a reusable carafe. Another promotion using specialty containers, recently used by the convenience store chain 7-11, consisted of "sound-off cups" that encouraged consumers to air their views on different issues by buying drinks in cups stating "Yes" or "No." Products sold in specialty containers usually carry the regular price, but if the container is unusually attractive the price of the product may be raised to cover part or all of the increased costs.

In addition to increasing sales of the product at the retail level, some reusable containers, such as coffee carafes, can encourage consumers to use the product more frequently in the future. (It is questionable, however, whether this will increase consumption for a particular brand rather than for all brands in the category.) Also, because specialty containers replace the regular packaging, that cost can be added to the value of the premium, allowing a better offer to be made.

The major problem with reusable containers is that if they are not the same size as the regular container or if they are fragile, they may present problems in handling, storing, and shelving at the retail level. Also, reusable containers that are unattractive to the consumer may actually result in decreased sales, particularly if they increase the price of the product.

Exhibit 5.8   A Reusable Container

Source: Courtesy of Paul Masson Wine.

Exhibit 5.9   A Reusable Container: Tang Breakfast Drink

Source: Courtesy of Kraft General Foods Corp.

Strategic Uses of Special Packs

Depending on the individual situation and how they are used, in-store premiums can be successful at gaining sales among a variety of consumers and, sometimes, at increasing future sales.

Exhibit 5.10 An In-Pack Premium Designed to Increase Consumption

Source: Courtesy of Campbell Soup Company.

Loyal Users

Current customers are probably the most likely to be affected by these types of "value-added" promotions. Bonus packs are very effective at loading loyal users with extra product, taking them out of the market for other brands (thereby providing a defense during periods when other products are likely to be promoting) and (with impulse products such as cookies) increasing consumption after purchase. Bonus packs, in-packs, on-packs, near-packs, and reusable containers can also make consumers more likely to buy more product; this can either encourage additional usage or change purchase timing by getting consumers to stock up.

Certain kinds of premiums (such as the Good Seasons salad dressing cruet) may also encourage more frequent usage of the product. And when in-pack, on-pack, or near-pack premiums consist of other products also sold individually by the same company, they can encourage crossover sales in the future among new customers who try and like them.

Competitive Loyals

Consumers who are brand-loyal to a competitive product because they think it's a slightly better deal, or because of inertia, sometimes may be influenced by an attractive in-pack, on-pack, or near-pack premium. (Bonus packs usually work less well for these people). For instance, a consumer who usually buys Amoco gasoline may decide to try Shell instead in order to pick up a stuffed animal for the kids. If this occurs, it is possible that the consumer will like the brand (or get accustomed to using it) and will continue to buy it after the promotion is over.

However, it should be noted that in order to persuade any competitive loyal, even one who purchases out of inertia, to buy another brand, a very attractive premium offer must be made. Many in-store premiums are therefore ignored by competitive loyals much of the time.

Switchers

Premium offers such as bonus packs, near-packs, in-packs, on-packs, and reusable containers can be very strong incentives to switchers, who may be easily influenced by the extra push that these kinds of items bring to the product. In categories where variety seeking is an issue, it sometimes may be helpful to include a sample of a similar product as the premium, in the hope that the next time the consumer switches it will be to that brand rather than to a competitive brand.

The one big negative associated with many in-packs, on-packs, near-packs, and specialty packages is the distribution issue. Because many retailers dislike the hassles involved with in-store premium offers, they often refuse to carry them. This may mean that premium offers, actually decrease distribution of the product. It is for this reason, and because of the increasing lack of power that manufacturers have over their distribution channels, that fewer companies offer premiums today than did in the past.

Price Buyers

Consumers who consistently buy the cheapest brand on the market will generally take advantage of a premium offer only if the item is of exceptional interest to them or if the price of the brand is relatively low. As with all promotions directed at price buyers, in-store premium offers should be expected to have little long-term residual value for the brand.

Exhibit 5.11   An In-Pack Attracting Switchers

Source: Courtesy of TDK.

Nonusers

Nonusers of a product category are even less likely to be attracted by premium offers than are competitive loyals. They certainly will not be influenced by the possibility of getting a larger amount of a type of product they never use, and they are also unlikely to be swayed by items offered through on-packs, in-packs, near-packs, and specialty packaging. Only if the premium is extremely attractive or not easily obtainable through other means, and if they already have some small interest in the product, are they likely to be influenced. For instance, it is conceivable that a person who never eats fast food might pick up a hamburger to obtain a poster from a special movie; however, this type of situation is likely to happen relatively infrequently and probably won't create much increased business after the promotion is over.

Special Packs and Residual Market Value

Bonus packs, in-packs, on-packs, near-packs, and specialty containers all make products more appealing to consumers. They appear to "reward" them for their purchases, thereby possibly generating positive feelings toward the brand. In addition, depending on what is being offered, premiums may sometimes cause people who don't usually buy—or never buy—a brand to try it. These people may then continue to use the product in the future.

Some premiums may also encourage consumers to use more product in the future (or make it easier for them to do so); other premiums may remind consumers of the brand or (when the premium is a T-shirt or other frequently displayed item featuring the product name) turn them into walking billboards for it. Finally, cross-ruffed premiums that consist of samples of other products made by the same manufacturer may cause people to try those brands, which may result in future demand for them.

CHAPTER SIX

Continuity Programs

C ontinuity programs are designed to create and reward brand loyalty among consumers who might otherwise switch from brand to brand within a category. They are especially popular in categories where consumer perception of product differentiation is low—a description that might apply to products as expensive as airline flights and as pedestrian as cornflakes.

Frequent-buyer programs are one of the fastest-growing forms of consumer promotions and have become especially popular among retailers. For example, by 1995 more than 70 percent of grocery retailers had established frequent buyer clubs for their customers. Another area where continuity programs have been successful is in the travel industry, with most airlines, hotel chains, and rental-car companies having established some kind of program. Although manufacturers who sell their products through retailers have been less proactive about pursuing continuity programs, most have participated in retailer frequent-buyer programs, and a few have experimented with their own programs.

Continuity programs have become successful for a number of reasons. A primary goal of such programs is to establish brand loyalty among consumers, particularly in categories where there is little product differentiation and switching is common. The rewards given to consumers in exchange for their business may also lead to goodwill among some consumers. In addition, frequent-buyer programs may help companies to build databases of people who have used their products and to learn which individuals are their best customers. These individuals then may receive special benefits in addition to the stated rewards of the program, leading to further brand loyalty.

Types of Continuity Programs

Continuity programs have become important tools for doing business in certain service industries, such as airlines (most now have some sort of frequent-flyer program) and hotels (with chains such as Hyatt now offering frequent-guest programs). These programs have been successful in providing consumers with an extra benefit in categories in which all brands generally offer similar prices and service levels. They have been especially popular with consumers who travel often on business (the largest and most profitable segment of the travel industry), largely because these people are able to use the rewards from the program for their own personal or vacation travel.

Frequent-traveler programs run by airlines, hotels, rental-car agencies, and other businesses generally give consumers a certain number of "points" for miles flown or visits made; these points can be exchanged for free services or upgrades in the future. Frequent-traveler clubs often offer special benefits to very frequent purchasers, such as automatic upgrades to first-class seating, more expensive cars or speedier check-ins, and the ability to accumulate points more quickly than other, less-valued customers.

Because frequent-flyer programs in particular have become so popular, many other kinds of companies have developed joint-venture programs with airlines to allow consumers to gain points in these programs, without ever leaving the ground, by purchasing unrelated products. In 1996, "miles" were available from several major airlines for about two cents each to any company wishing to offer them to customers. Firms that have offered "miles" to their customers in recent years have included credit-card issuers, long-distance telephone companies, hotels and rental-car agencies, lawn-care services, restaurants, furniture stores, investment brokers, roofing companies, and even charitable organizations solicit donations. Conversely, airlines have developed programs that allow some of their frequent flyers to use their accumulated mileage for benefits other than airline travel, such as tickets to sporting events or magazine subscriptions.

Spurred on by the success of frequent-traveler clubs, many other kinds of businesses have begun using databases to establish their own frequent-buyer clubs. For example, Waldenbooks (its sales threatened in many markets by discount-priced rivals) uses a program where, for a small annual fee, members are entitled to automatic discounts on merchandise and receive store credits through the mail for every $100 spent. As a side benefit, the chain was able to develop a list of its customers and their buying behaviors for use in future marketing efforts.

A number of credit-card companies also have initiated continuity plans for their cardholders by offering "bonus points" that can be used toward purchases of discounted merchandise by customers charging purchases on their cards. Another company that has been successful at implementing a continuity program is the Book-of-the-Month Club, which has offered points that can be applied to purchases of older, overstocked titles. A variety of other merchants, such as florists, coffee shops, and restaurants, have also offered continuity programs giving free or reduced-priced merchandise to "Frequent Flower Buyers," "Frequent Sippers," or "Frequent Diners."

Exhibit 6.1   Store Continuity Program

Source: Courtesy of Jewel Food Stores.

The business that seems to have demonstrated the most rapid growth in recent years in terms of its usage of continuity programs, however, is grocery retailing. Supermarkets have long used continuity programs to distinguish themselves from competitors, of course, from the use of trading stamps that could be exchanged for free merchandise in the 1960s and 1970s to more recent programs that gave consumers a free Thanksgiving turkey if they purchased a specific amount of groceries over a given period of time. Another popular retailer program offers a series of items to consumers, each of which must be acquired individually on different shopping occasions. For example, this type of continuity program may allow consumers to obtain a new volume in a cookbook set, or a new pan in a set of cookware each week by shopping a particular supermarket. Obviously, these programs are designed to keep consumers returning to the store in order to collect the complete set of items.

Exhibit 6.2   Continuity Program: Post Cereal

Source: William A. Robinson, *100 Best Sales Promotions of 1976/77* (Chicago: Crain Books, 1977), p.27.

Exhibit 6.3 A Continuity Program for a Packaged-Goods Product

Source: Courtesy of Philip Morris.

Most recently, grocery retailers have turned to frequent-shopper programs in an attempt to differentiate themselves from competition and increase consumer loyalty. While many of these programs merely give consumers discounts on their current purchases, they also have the potential for providing discounts based on purchases over time. The main obstacle facing grocery retailers in developing such programs is that these retailers tend to operate on low margins and therefore have a relatively small amount of money to give back to consumers as rewards. Most of the discounts on current purchases awarded to consumers who belong to store clubs are subsidized by manufacturers through trade deals, but gathering enough funds to give consumers meaningful rewards for their purchases over time seems to have proven more challenging for retailers.

While most packaged-goods companies that market products through retailers have made limited attempts to establish continuity programs, a few have created their own successful frequent-buyer promotions. Pepsi-Cola, for instance, created a program called Pepsi Stuff in which consumers collected award points to obtain various items. The initial program turned out to be so popular that Pepsi had to curtail its advertising so its merchandise supply was not exhausted. Other mass marketers of products in categories where purchases are frequent and switching is common, such as diaper manufacturers and cigarette companies, have established similar programs. Although such programs require significant expense and effort to plan and administer, they will probably become more prevalent in the future, as more mass marketers become interested in pursuing database marketing programs directly with consumers.

Issues in Developing Continuity Programs

Continuity programs have a number of advantages. They can be successful in increasing loyalty for a particular product, especially in situations where products are purchased frequently and where real or perceived differences among products are slight. Continuity programs can take consumers out of the market for competitive products, and they may in some cases make consumers feel better about the product being purchased. They also can help the marketer to compile a list of the company's most valued customers; these people can then be targeted with intensive selling messages later on. In addition, continuity programs, like refunds, may have considerable slippage, since many people may sign up for the program but then fail to claim their rewards.

However, continuity programs also have a number of disadvantages. They usually must run for a long period of time, so they require a major commitment from the marketer. These programs also present a large legal liability for the marketer. Consumers must also be willing to make a commitment to doing business with the firm over a long period of time to get the rewards, and they may become impatient while waiting to obtain desired items.

Continuity programs may also be ineffective for inexpensive or infrequently purchased products, since they can be expensive to administer and since the lag time before an attractive reward can be given is likely to be unrealistically long. Taco Bell, for example, has experimented with a "Border Passport" frequent rewards club, which employed a swipe card to dispense free food, soft drinks, and gifts to frequent customers. Although the program was successful at getting younger consumers to visit Taco Bell restaurants more often and to switch to higher-priced menu items, it also created a number of problems, including slowing down service during busy time periods.

Another problem with continuity plans is that they may create large liabilities for companies that use accounting methods which require them to treat all benefits of such programs as though they will actually be cashed in. For this reason, some companies have instituted expiration dates on the use of the benefits, thereby reducing permanent liabilities in the program.

Another important point for marketers to keep in mind is that establishing a continuity program is not an appropriate substitute for attempting to create brand loyalty in other ways. While continuity programs are usually designed to prevent switching, it should be noted that the brand loyalty they create is not to the actual product, but rather to the rewards being obtained. In fact, frequent-buyer programs may even cause consumers to wonder about the merits of the products they are purchasing. For instance, at one point Breeze detergent ran a continuity program giving away towels in each box. However, it may have been unclear to consumers whether they bought the brand because they liked the product or because of the free towels. Once the towels were no longer being given away, or when consumers had enough towels and didn't want any more, it was questionable whether they would continue to buy the brand.

This problem has become apparent even in industries where continuity programs are an extremely important element of doing business. Some marketing managers, for instance, believe that because all airlines offer basically the same benefits to their members, frequent-flyer clubs have ceased to be a differentiating factor and instead are now a cost of doing business. Therefore, companies that use frequent-buyer promotions should continue to pursue other ways to create brand loyalty and avoid taking the customers enrolled in these programs for granted.

Planning Continuity Programs

Because continuity programs require a major investment in time and money, it can be helpful for manufacturers to consult a professional organization that specializes in this field. Usually, such programs are fairly complex, require a great deal of handling, and can be quite risky if not properly planned. Here are some general areas that should be given particular attention:

1. *Objectives of the continuity program.* Will the program run for a short period of time and offer a number of coupons or proofs of purchase for obtaining one specific item, or will it be an ongoing program in which several prizes or gifts are available over time? Each has a different set of objectives, costs, and sales promotion implementations.

2. *Type of proof of purchase required.* Some products or packages lend themselves well to providing a proof of purchase or label, and in some situations, such as the airline industry, the company itself may keep track of the purchases. In other cases, however, deciding how to keep track of purchases is not so simple. For instance, getting a proof of purchase from a plastic or metal container is often nearly impossible. Also, though many companies provide their customers with punch cards or electronic "smart" cards that keep track of purchases, many consumers already carry a great many items in their wallets and may not relish the opportunity to participate in a club that requires them to add another card to their collection. Therefore, marketers who can create data-based systems to record information about purchases for consumers may find their promotions more successful at attracting participants.

3. *Number and cost of premiums.* This is obviously a key element in the success of any continuity program. If the prize structure is limited to one item, has it been pre-tested for consumer acceptance? A program offering a prize or a gift with little or no appeal is worse than no program at all.

What will be the cost of the premiums? Some of the most successful rewards are items that are valuable to consumers but can be supplied at a nominal cost to the marketer. For example, frequent-flyer programs reward consumers with airline seats that might otherwise have gone empty. Overstocked or out-of-season merchandise can also make an attractive but inexpensive premium, as demonstrated by the Book-of-the-Month Club. Finally, what about the availability of prizes? Nothing upsets consumers more than to save for a gift and then find that it's not available.

4. *Structure of the program.* Will only proofs of purchase be accepted, or may cash be substituted for some of them? If the premium is to be packed in the product, will this create problems with production or distribution?

5. *Duration of the offer.* How long will the continuity program run? The time period of the offer must be long enough so that the average consumer will be able to make sufficient purchases to obtain the gift. If there is no initial time limit, there will be consumer resistance if an attempt is made to institute a deadline later on.

6. *Handling the fulfillment of the offer.* How will the prize or gift be distributed—through stores, through the mail? Who is to accept the orders, check them, and distribute the premiums?

All of the above questions and many others must be answered in the process of setting up a continuity plan. Therefore it can often be helpful to contact organizations specializing in these kinds of activities.

Strategic Uses of Continuity Programs

As previously stated, a continuity program can be successful in building brand loyalty during the length of the promotion and in warding off competitive threats. The main issues with this kind of program are in finding rewards that will be attractive to consumers and that will correspond to budgetary constraints, and in getting consumers to begin and to continue to participate in the program.

Loyal Users

Continuity programs are often helpful in allowing companies to capitalize on their current customers. Loyal users are relatively likely to enroll in a continuity program, since they usually purchase the brand anyway; once enrolled, they become even less likely to be lured away by competitors' promotional activities.

Also, in certain situations consumers may be tempted to buy more of a particular product in order to gain points that bring them closer to a reward, or to obtain a certain desired item in a series promotion. Finally, in situations where a number of products are tied together into one continuity program, crossover sales may occur as users of one type of product try others in order to obtain points to be used toward getting the prize. If that occurs and if consumers like the products they sample, then they may continue to buy them even after the promotion is over.

Competitive Loyals

Continuity programs are much less effective at addressing competitive loyals than are most sales promotion programs. Most competitive loyals will be unwilling to make a commitment to buying another brand on a regular basis. Only those consumers who are loyal mostly because of inertia and who are attracted by a particularly good reward are likely to even consider participating in a continuity program.

Switchers

Switchers are very likely to be influenced on their purchasing decisions by continuity programs. Continuity programs provide a point of differentiation to consumers, which often may succeed in creating brand loyalty to a particular product. Although some switchers may get accustomed to using a particular product and continue to do so after the promotion is over, most of this increased brand loyalty will last only as long as the continuity program.

Switchers who use multiple brands because they enjoy the variety, however, are unlikely to commit themselves to a continuity program. It may be for this reason that continuity programs are used in few categories where variety is a motivator.

Price Buyers

Unless the reward is particularly desirable, price buyers are unlikely to be tempted by continuity programs, since getting a good deal on the purchase price is usually a more important motivator to these people than obtaining a free gift sometime in the future. Only if the price is competitive and rewards are large will they be likely to commit to a program.

Nonusers

Continuity programs are unlikely to have any effect on nonusers of the product category. If people are not using any product in the category, then they are unlikely to anticipate that they will start using it often enough in the future to obtain the reward, no matter how attractive it might be.

Continuity Programs and Residual Value

In certain circumstances, continuity programs can be very effective in reducing switching and getting consumers to stick with a particular brand. However, whether these promotions actually have any effect on brand equity—that is, on consumers' perceptions of the brand and on their willingness to buy the product after the continuity program is over—is often doubtful.

Continuity programs usually do not make consumers more aware of the inherent benefits of a brand; instead they offer a reward (or a "bribe") to get consumers to buy the product repeatedly over an extended period of time. One problem with this is that if the continuity program is successful, it may be easily matched by other companies. As a result, profit margins may be lowered throughout the industry. In addition, consumers may get used to obtaining the rewards of continuity programs, meaning that such programs can often be extremely difficult to discontinue. In many cases, too, continuity programs may distract attention from service or product quality, and, in the long run, increase the number of consumers who buy only because of price or "deals."

In some cases, however, continuity programs have the potential of allowing marketers to learn more about their customers and to market to them more effectively. For instance, Waldenbooks' frequent-reader club allows the company to keep track of each individual's purchases; this information can then be used to promote other products to these consumers. For example, frequent buyers of cookbooks might be sent a special newsletter describing new cookbooks in detail, or might be invited to attend a special seminar hosted by the author of a new cookbook. Although most marketers offering continuity programs have only begun to use information in this way, these types of promotions have the potential of providing consumers with added benefits or of increasing sales volume among specific segments of the population.

Continuity programs often may be most advantageous to the larger firms in the industry. When consumers are forced to choose between competing companies' programs, they may select the brand that seems most convenient. For instance, they may choose the airline with the most flights, the hotel chain with the most locations, the bookstore closest to home, or, in the case of packaged goods, the brand they already use most often, which will usually be the brand with the biggest market share. This may mean that, if all the competitors in an industry institute continuity programs, some switchers may cease purchasing products or services from the smaller players. Therefore the smaller marketers in an industry should think long and hard before they begin continuity programs, even if those programs seem likely to be advantageous in the short run.

In fact, because of the issues involved, all marketers who are considering instituting continuity programs need to think carefully about what they are hoping to accomplish and about whether they are willing to commit to the program for the long term. Companies that are simply hoping to perk up short-term profits should probably look to other types of promotions to accomplish that goal.

CHAPTER SEVEN

Refunds

In a way, refunds can be viewed as coupons that offer delayed gratification to the consumer. Refund offers allow consumers to buy a product and then, later on, to get back a portion of the purchase price.

However, while the popularity of coupons has grown dramatically since the early 1980s, the usage of refunds has been declining. For example, in 1995 only 66 percent of surveyed manufacturers reported having used refunds over the past year, compared to 77 percent in 1991. Some possible reasons for this decline include the low appeal of rebates to consumers who want immediate gratification, and the rising postage costs that have made the mechanics of getting refunds to customers less attractive to both consumers and manufacturers.

Uses of Refunds

A refund (or rebate) is simply an offer by a manufacturer to return a certain amount of money to the consumer when a particular product or group of products is purchased. Although refunds are usually delivered to consumers through the mail, in some cases (such as with automobiles) they may be given to individuals at the point of purchase.

Although refund offers originated in the food business, they are often used today on more expensive items, such as over-the-counter drugs, electronics, health-care and beauty-care products, liquor, appliances, and automobiles. Refunds have been especially popular on these types of products because they enable the manufacturer to deliver to the consumer a substantial discount without the major misredemption problems that can often accompany the use of high-value coupons.

Although refunds are still used occasionally on low-priced products, there are several reasons why they are used less often today. First, postage rates have increased, meaning that a refund of 50 cents or $1 is likely to be perceived as hardly worthwhile by both the consumer (who must mail in a proof of purchase with a request for the refund) and by the manufacturer (who must mail checks to consumers). In addition, many consumers have become brand switchers and are less likely now to purchase eight tubes of toothpaste to acquire a $2 refund. Finally, because manufacturer margins are low on most grocery items, it is difficult to make an attractive refund offer to consumers on these low-priced products.

Exhibit 7.1   Refund: Purchase of One Product

Source: William A. Robinson, *100 Best Sales Promotions* (Chicago: Crain Books, 1980), p. 115.

High-value refunds may occasionally be used effectively, however, on new packaged-goods products or on brands with low market shares. They also may be effective on products being introduced into new geographic areas.

Refunds may also be used effectively on brands priced higher than the competition, in order to induce trial without a price cut. For example, Bailey's Irish Cream liqueur, a premium brand in the category, once used a rebate to get first-time buyers of Irish cream liqueurs to sample Bailey's rather than a competitive product.

Since refunds tend to be most attractive when they are for relatively large amounts of money, they are particularly effective in generating trial for fairly expensive, high-margin products that are purchased frequently by consumers, such as batteries, pet food, or liquor. Because these products are costly, a large rebate may be offered; and because they are purchased frequently, consumers who decide they like the brand may purchase it often in the future.

Refunds may also be effective in getting consumers to buy slow-moving, parity-type, impulse products that are used up quickly. Refunds also work well in product categories where there is not a constant barrage of sales promotion activities or media advertising.

Direct-to-consumer refunds are also appropriate for products such as athletic shoes, contact lenses, videotapes, or appliances, which are distributed through retailers other than supermarkets or drugstores. Since the retailers that carry these products often do not accept coupons, refunds can provide a good way for manufacturers to give a discount on their product directly to consumers.

Refunds are often used by manufacturers because they attract attention to brands at the point of purchase at relatively low expense. There is evidence to suggest that consumers who take advantage of refund offers may be better able to remember the brand than with other offers. In addition, manufacturers may benefit from slippage, which occurs when consumers buy the product and plan to take advantage of the rebate but neglect to send for it. Slippage rates with refund offers may be considerable, averaging 20 percent in the grocery products category.

In cases where more than one purchase must be made to get the refund, this type of sales promotion can load some consumers with product, making it more difficult for competitors to make immediate sales and sometimes getting consumers accustomed to purchasing a particular brand. Products flagged with refund offers may also attract attention at the point of purchase and may occasionally help to get in-store displays for brands.

Another advantage of refunds is that they may sometimes prompt response from consumers who are not affected by coupons. According to Manufacturer's Coupon Control Center, 44 percent of nonusers of coupons claim to have sent in a proof of purchase in order to obtain a refund check. And because refunds require consumers to supply their names and addresses, this type of promotion can be helpful to companies wishing to establish customer databases.

Exhibit 7.2   A Refund on a Product Purchased Through a Non-Grocery Retailer

Source: Courtesy of CIBA Vision Corporation.

As previously mentioned, however, refunds have a number of disadvantages. Rising postage costs have made it less worthwhile for consumers to submit their proofs of purchase and for companies to mail checks to consumers. Busy consumers may be turned off by the trouble of mailing in their requests for refunds and by the need to purchase more than one item; they may also be discouraged by the need to wait weeks for the refund to arrive. Some consumers may submit proofs of purchase from items bought before the refund offer, meaning that the company can end up giving discounts on items that have already been sold.

In short, although refunds can be appropriate for some products and some situations, their effects on sales are usually much less observable than those of coupons.

Types of Refunds

Refunds may be offered on a single purchase of a product or on multiple purchases. Increasingly, though, manufacturers are structuring their rebate programs so that only one purchase needs to be made to obtain the rebate. This type of promotion addresses consumers' increasing desire for quick gratification, and it can result in relatively high response rates.

With low-priced products, such as groceries or health-care items, this strategy may mean that the entire purchase price (or most of it) must be refunded if the promotion is to be attractive to consumers. Obviously, companies that refund such a large amount are focused on the long term, such as the effort to create trial for a new product in a competitive, high-margin category. And, in many cases, this kind of refund may act as a selective sampling program targeted toward consumers who, because they must go to the trouble of searching for the product and sending for the refund, are more interested than the rest of population in the product category. Like most brand-building sales-promotion activities, this type of refund offer works best for brands that offer equal or better quality or value than the competition and have previously been sampled by a relatively small percentage of the target market.

More expensive products, such as durable goods, have the luxury of offering rebates on single products even after the initial trial period, in order to attract consumer attention and provide a sales boost for the brand. In the case of high-priced items, such as automobiles, rebates may total $1,000 to $2,000 or more. More modestly, makers of some higher-priced packaged goods, such as

Butterball turkeys, may pay $1 to $2 refunds in exchange for a single proof of purchase.

Refunds may also be made on multiple purchases of the same brand, although this kind of offer is less popular than in the past. This type of rebate generally fails to attract new customers to a particular product, since people are unlikely to risk purchasing several packages of a brand they haven't tried before.

Refunds made on multiple purchases of a brand tend to be used in categories where product is purchased often and brand loyalty is low, resulting in frequent switching. For instance, an orange juice manufacturer may offer a refund of $1 on six cans of frozen juice.

Exhibit 7.3   Refund Offer: Purchase of Paired Products

Source: Courtesy of Carr's Crackers.

Occasionally, a manufacturer may choose to tie several products together into a single rebate offer. This type of rebate may be more cost-efficient to distribute to the consumer, and may give a boost to weaker products in the line. In addition, requiring the purchase of several products may allow an attractive rebate to be made. However, this type of refund offer usually has a lower response rate than others, because consumers may not be interested in purchasing all the products being promoted. Therefore, many refund promotions give consumers a choice of products to purchase. For example, Procter and Gamble may link all of its personal-care products together in an offer that allows consumers to get $3 back if they buy several of the items. Another way to make this type of offer attractive to a wide variety of consumers, yet still obtain the advantages of a multiproduct offer, is to take a tiered approach: for example, "Buy one of these items and get $1 back; buy both and get $3 back."

Exhibit 7.4   A Refund on the Purchase of One Product

Source: Courtesy of Smith-Kline Beecham.

Marketers may occasionally choose to run a refund offer with their own brand and another related product in order to attract consumer attention and suggest a use for the brand. If the related product is a brand made by another manufacturer, the two companies might split the cost of the promotion. For instance, Hershey's chocolate, Keebler graham crackers, and Kraft marshmallows might team up in a refund program encouraging consumers to make S'Mores, a popular dessert sandwich. By encouraging expanded usage of the products, the promotion might result in increased sales at a fairly low cost for each of the three manufacturers.

Other promotions pair a particular brand with a related generic item, such as Oreo cookies and vanilla ice cream. The idea here is either to suggest new usage ideas that may be repeated in the future or simply to promote trial of one product by giving consumers a "deal" on something they would have purchased anyway. For instance, Carr's crackers, a high-quality, low-share brand, offered consumers a $2 refund when they purchased two packages of crackers and "your favorite cheese."

Refunds and Other Sales Promotions

Refunds can often provide a boost to other types of sales promotion activities. For instance, coupons distributed to consumers may be accompanied by refund offers; the combination of the immediate and long-term incentives to purchase may prove to be attractive. Another method is to send coupons to customers who have requested a rebate; this may help to reinforce the initial purchase and possibly make the consumer more likely to buy the brand again in the future. ("Bounce-back" coupons of this type are usually very successful, sometimes achieving redemption rates of 80 percent or more.) In addition, if the coupon is mentioned in the original materials describing the refund offer, it may cause more people to respond.

Rebates may also be used effectively in conjunction with sweepstakes. Although consumers may not be required to make a purchase to enter a sweepstakes, some manufacturers have successfully structured their promotions so that consumers who mail in refund claims are entered automatically. This may increase the likelihood that consumers will actually buy the product rather than just sending in their names, as happens in many sweepstakes.

Exhibit 7.5   Refund and Coupons: Ziploc Offer

Source: Courtesy of DowBrands.

Another way that rebates may be used is as a "guarantee" to consumers who have not used the product before. Typically, consumers are offered a cash or check refund if they don't like the product, or the opportunity to obtain coupons for more product if they do like it. For instance, users of food storage bags were invited to judge how easy it was to close Ziploc bags compared to their regular brand. Those who chose their original brand received $2.25 in cash; those picking Ziploc got an equal amount in coupons for future Ziploc purchases. (To make consumers more likely to request the coupon, however, and to make them more likely to tell themselves that the challenger is really better than their current brand, the value of the coupons is often set at a much greater amount than that of the cash.) In addition to generating trial, the Ziploc promotion encouraged consumers to actively notice and examine one of the brand's benefits, making it more likely that they will buy the product in the future.

Exhibit 7.6   A Refund Offer Guaranteeing Satisfaction

Source: Courtesy of General Mills.

Consumer Usage

Although all demographic groups tend to be aware of refund offers, and although many consumers who don't use coupons do occasionally take advantage of them, coupon users tend to be the heaviest users of rebates. Larger households, heavy coupon users, traditional single-income families, and women are also likely to be heavy users of refunds, according to the Manufacturer's Coupon Control Center.

Refund Offer Development

Refund promotions themselves are usually not difficult to set up, and they can often be initiated rather quickly. However, since refund offers can be expensive and amounts being refunded can be quite large, a good system of control over the technique is a must. For example, computer software programs are available that ascertain that individuals obtain only one refund each and that proofs of purchase are valid.

A major factor in the success of a refund offer is the fulfillment procedure. Usually, this is best handled by a fulfillment organization that is set up to handle redemption programs. Typical costs for a refund offer fulfillment in 1990 were approximately $3.20 per thousand replies received. The marketer pays the fulfillment organization on the basis of the number of replies received and filled as a result of the promotion.

For example, assume a manufacturer offers a $2 refund for three proofs of purchase. The consumer sends the three proofs along with the refund offer form to the fulfillment organization, which checks to make certain that the requirements are met and mails the check or cash to the consumer. The fulfillment house then bills the advertiser for the actual orders filled; that is, if 20,000 orders are received, the fulfillment house bills the advertiser $64 ($3.20 per thousand × 20,000 responses). In most cases the fulfillment house would be responsible for the costs of the return card and the envelope and of addressing the refund. The postage might or might not be included, depending on the rate used. The marketer would, of course, also provide the fulfillment house with the $40,000 in refunds to be sent to the consumers.

One opportunity that marketers should not overlook is the ability to use fulfillment of the refund to further promote the product to the consumer. Too often, consumers receive rebate checks that state only the name of the fulfillment house, with no clue as to what product purchase actually prompted the refund payment. Since consumers are likely to feel positive about receiving a refund check, however, it is likely that if the sponsoring brand is named, some of that good feeling may rub off onto the product itself. Materials that might be included with the refund check include coupons for the same product or for other products made by the same manufacturer (especially appropriate since responders to refund offers are likely to use coupons) or a simple "Thank you" for the purchase.

Redemption

Traditionally, redemption of refund offers has been about 1 to 2 percent of the media circulation of the offer. For example, if the refund offer were made in newspapers with a combined circulation of 1,000,000, then refunds should not exceed 10,000 to 20,000.

Refund redemption rates do vary by media, however. Generally, the closer the offer is to the actual product, the higher the redemption rate—for example, on-pack refund offers do better than tear-off pads, which do better than media offers. However, it is not absolutely certain which of these techniques is best at creating new sales for the brand; it may be, for instance, that on-pack offers are more often noticed and used by people who would have purchased the product anyway.

Redemption rates can often be improved through the use of other promotional techniques. Media advertising, point-of-purchase materials, and, especially, "flags" on the front of the product itself can all cause more consumers to take advantage of the rebate offer.

One of the major advantages of refund offers is their flexibility. The number of refunds made may be increased or decreased by varying three factors:

1. The value of the refund may be raised or lowered. If a refund of $2 is presently being used, activity can be increased by offering a $3 refund. Of course, lowering the refund value reduces the redemptions.

2. The number of proofs of purchase required can be raised or lowered. By increasing the number, redemptions can be reduced.

By lowering the requirements, the number of redemptions will increase.

3. By varying the ways the offer is advertised, the number of refunds can be increased or decreased.

Costs

In addition to the value of the refund itself, several other costs are incurred in a refund offer:

- Media advertising to support the offer.

- Point-of-purchase materials, order pads, or other display materials for use at retail.

- Handling fees by the fulfillment house; postage, envelopes, labor, and related costs.

- If a coupon is used, the clearinghouse fees for handling, plus the usual handling fee to the retailer.

To estimate the cost of a refund offer, manufacturers must first determine the actual costs involved, including additional handling or other fees, and then compare the number to the estimated return. For example, assume that a marketer is making a purchase price refund on a package of rice that retails for 69 cents. In addition to the refund price of 69 cents, the fulfillment organization would charge the marketer approximately $3.00 for each 1,000 refunds received and returned, plus the cost of postage and supplies (such as envelopes and forms).

Rules

Perhaps the most important factor in presenting the refund offer is making the rules clear. A checklist for marketers conducting refund offers includes:

- Keep the offer simple.

- State clearly how many proofs of purchase are required.

- Require the standard proof of purchase—nothing esoteric.

- Require the respondent's zip code.

- Allow four weeks for delivery.

- Choose shorter expiration dates for media offers and longer ones for offers made on point-of-purchase materials and in-pack or on-pack.

- Put the expiration date in bold type and make it easy to find.

- Limit the refund offer to one per family.

Strategic Uses of Refunds

Obviously, some consumers never respond to any refund offer, whereas others respond to many offers. For consumers who are prone to respond to refund offers, however, the value of this kind of promotion can vary depending on the objectives that have been developed.

Loyal Users

Loyal users are the consumers most likely to take advantage of refund offers. Although current users may take advantage of refund offers, it is questionable whether these promotions will actually result in overall increased profits, especially since the values of many refunds tend to be quite large in comparison to the overall price of the product being sold.

Certain refund offers may have a moderate effect on coaxing extra sales from current customers. This may work with infrequently purchased, impulse-type items. For example, a consumer who occasionally drinks single-malt Scotch may notice a refund offer on the bottle and decide to purchase the Scotch as a special treat. In addition, purchase timing may also be affected by refund offers. For instance, a loyal driver of a Honda Accord may purchase a new model a year earlier than planned if an attractive manufacturer rebate is offered.

Another situation where extra sales might be gained from current customers is with promotions where multiple purchases must be made in order to obtain the refund. Consumers might stock up on the product in order to be able to claim the refund. This is likely to be most beneficial in categories where extra product purchased is likely to be quickly consumed, as may be the case with items such as ice cream. (Incidentally, if the extra product is *not* going to be quickly consumed, then it is necessary to make the proof of purchase easy to remove from the package while it still contains the product. For example, if consumers must buy five boxes of facial tissue to obtain a refund, and they have to cut holes in the boxes before they're opened to get the proofs to send in, they are likely to become annoyed at both the process and the company.) Refund offers that link two products may be successful at getting loyal users of one product to try another product made by the same manufacturer. As mentioned earlier, however, this type of strategy may ultimately result in low overall redemption rates.

Competitive Loyals

Like most sales promotion activities, refunds are unlikely to influence consumers who are intensely loyal to a competitive product. However, because they often offer consumers a fairly large discount on the purchase price, refunds frequently can be more successful than many other promotions at getting moderately loyal consumers of other brands to try a competing product. This may be especially true when refunds are flagged on the package at the point of purchase, attracting attention at the moment when the consumer is about to buy another brand. On the other hand, competitive users are less likely to save a refund offer from mass media and then remember to buy the product, unless their loyalty to their current brand is already weak.

It is worth noting that the large refund offers needed to attract competitive loyals are likely to be even more attractive to consumers who have sometimes or always purchased the product in the past, and who might well have purchased it again without the refund offer. This means that large refunds can often result in immediate, substantial financial losses in profitability. Thus, higher-value refunds are offered mostly on new or low-share brands where competitive users make up most of the population.

Switchers

Refunds may often be successful at getting consumers to purchase one brand rather than another for reasons related to value or variety. They may be effective tools when the product is of relatively high value and when sales will be profitable even after the refund is made to the consumer. In this case the goal is simply to create short-term sales rather than to prompt an increase in long-term value, so whether the switcher buys the brand on a consistent basis in the future is less important.

Refunds that amount to a large percentage of the manufacturer's profit margin on the product should not usually be used to generate sales from switchers, however. Obviously, consumers who have purchased the product in the past but continue to buy other brands are unlikely to become much more brand loyal because of one trial, even though they are very likely to take advantage of an attractive refund offer.

Although they may give the sales force "something to talk about" with the trade, refunds probably are less successful than other sales promotion tactics at obtaining and maintaining retail distribution. Refund offers distributed through mass media tend to have low response rates, meaning that few customers enter the store looking for the product and complaining to retailers if it is not available.

Price Buyers

Price buyers are probably the people most likely to take advantage of a big rebate offer; however, they are unlikely to continue to buy the product at full price after the rebate is over. Therefore marketers planning refund programs with high values should find out how many price buyers exist in the category. Running high-value refund offers in categories where a large percentage of consumers are price buyers is likely to be more expensive and less successful at increasing purchases over the long term than making similar offers in categories that are less price-sensitive.

Nonusers

Occasionally, nonusers of a particular category might be persuaded to try a particular brand if a rebate is large enough; they then may decide they like the product and purchase it again in the future. This is especially true in new product categories. However, because nonusers of products usually do not even notice promotional materials for those products and generally have reasons for not using them, they are unlikely to take advantage of most refund offers.

Exhibit 7.7 A Refund Offer Attracting New Users to the Category

Source: Courtesy of Ciba-Geigy Corporation.

Refunds and Residual Market Value

When used appropriately, refund offers can have a considerable positive effect on the value of the brand. A high-value rebate offer can persuade consumers to try a product; if they like it, they may very well buy it again. However, this kind of brand-building activity is likely to come at the expense of short-run profits, and is therefore most appropriately used by companies trying to build market share for new products or for products currently used by a relatively small percentage of the population. The residual value of this sort of rebate tends to be greatest when the product being promoted has a demonstrable benefit over others in the category, and when it is likely to be used often in the future.

A second way in which refunds may create value is when a promotion that requires multiple purchases of a brand helps to get consumers used to buying a particular product; it may then be more likely that these people will continue to buy it in the future. However, consumers who are willing to make multiple purchases in order to obtain a refund are probably more promotion-sensitive than the rest of the population, and so they also may be likely to be tempted by other companies' promotions in the future.

CHAPTER EIGHT

Sweepstakes and Contests

S weepstakes and contests are generally used by marketers as attention-getters or excitement-builders, or as tie-ins to some type of event or activity. In addition, because many forms of sweepstakes or contests require consumers to submit their names and addresses in order to enter, they also can be useful for firms attempting to build databases of their customers.

Although consumers may lump contests and sweepstakes into one category, the law makes strong distinctions between the two. Winners in sweepstakes are determined solely by chance, whereas contests require entrants to demonstrate some sort of skill (such as writing a poem or answering a series of questions). Understanding this distinction is important because while consumers from most states who enter a contest may be required to make a purchase of a product, U.S. law requires that sweepstakes be open to non-buyers as well as buyers.

Sweepstakes or Contest?

Although sweepstakes have traditionally been much more popular than contests among marketers, an increasing number of contests have been conducted in recent years. About 44 percent of surveyed packaged-goods product manufacturers reported using contests during 1995, compared to 63 percent who used sweepstakes.

A primary advantage of sweepstakes is that they attract many more entrants than contests—often more than ten times as many. Sweepstakes tend to be popular with consumers because they require no skill (giving the impression that anyone can win) and are easier to enter. In addition, because sweepstakes target a broader base of consumers, they usually offer larger prizes.

Contests, on the other hand, have a number of advantages that account for their rising popularity:

- Contests can require a purchase in most states in the United States, and therefore often attract people who have some interest in the products being promoted. On the other hand, sweepstakes often attract many "professional entrants" (peo-

Exhibit 8.1   A Contest Encouraging a High Amount of Product Involvement

Source: Courtesy of Heinz.

ple who spend a great deal of time entering contests) who make no purchase and often have no interest in the product category.

- Because contests require some kind of skill, most people enter only once or a few times. On the other hand, sweepstakes contestants often send in multiple entries. While companies technically can attempt to limit such entries to one per person or household, screening thousands or millions of entries to make certain that no duplicates are received is often impossible.

- Because consumers feel they have some control over the outcome of contests, they sometimes put a great deal of effort into perfecting their entries. Contests therefore may attract more attention and interest than sweepstakes, which often provoke a relatively low level of involvement among the people who enter them.

- Contests can often be designed to have public relations value. For example, Ben & Jerry's received a great deal of publicity for a contest that let individuals apply to be the new CEO of the company by sending in an essay or poem describing their qualifications. (While a candidate proposed by a headhunter was eventually chosen, the contest reinforced the ice cream company's down-home image and drew public attention to the executive who was selected.) Other contests often receive media attention simply because of their amusement value. For example, a contest seeking talking dogs, called "Teach Your Dog to Say Pasta," helped to publicize its sponsor—Thompson's Pet Pasta Products—through a number of media mentions.

- Contests sometimes allow companies to solve marketing problems—or at least to make consumers feel they have the opportunity to be a part of the process. Microsoft, for example, ran a contest for students to propose ideas for "what the coolest computer could do." Winners got a trip to Microsoft's headquarters, where they discussed their proposals over lunch with company founder Bill Gates. Kibbles 'n Bits ran a promotion encouraging dog owners to show what their dog would do to get some of the dog food; winners appeared in commercials for the product.

Exhibit 8.2   A Contest Designed to Solve a
Marketing Problem

Source: Courtesy of James B. Beam Distilling Co.

Exhibit 8.3   A Contest Auditioning Dogs for a Commercial

Source: Courtesy of Heinz Pet Products.

Despite these advantages, contests may be most appropriately used to address particular marketing problems, such as targeting a specialized group of consumers that might actually be interested in the competition. For instance, sailboat enthusiasts might enjoy participating in a sailing contest, and *Star Trek* fans might be willing to show off their knowledge of the show by participating in a trivia contest.

Contests also may be more successful when entering is not too difficult for consumers. For instance, Vienna Beef frankfurters once ran a contest encouraging consumers to write an advertising slogan for the product, but the winner turned out to be a professional advertising copywriter. (The publicity that the company gained from the contest may have made the promotion worthwhile, however.) On the other hand, Wendy's hamburger chain felt reasonably confident about running a contest to find look-alikes of its founder, Dave Thomas, since many people had previously written the company stating that they had an uncle or neighbor who was a dead ringer for him.

Sales Force Contests

The most successful contests are often conducted not at the consumer level, but instead are designed to encourage company, distributor, or retail sales forces to work harder to sell the product. For instance, a manufacturer of expensive luggage may reward its top salesperson at the retail level with a new automobile. Or, a company selling computers might reward its entire sales force with a trip to Hawaii if they sell a predetermined number of machines during a certain period in time.

Another related form of promotion is the use of spiffs, which reward retail- or distributor-level salespeople with a certain amount of cash for each item they sell. Retail spiffs are usually offered on relatively high-value products, such as appliances; distributor-level spiffs may be offered either on individual products or on cases of inexpensive products. Although retailer spiffs can be quite successful in getting salespeople to work to persuade consumers to buy a particular brand, they may be frowned upon by some retailers who believe that they reduce sales force credibility among the store's customers, who may rely on salespeople to make unbiased product recommendations.

Another contest used to motivate salespeople at the retail level is the "mystery shopper" approach, a promotion that is announced to retailers in advance. Mystery shoppers usually consist of actors, hired by manufacturers, who visit retail outlets asking for assistance and recommendations. If salespeople respond by suggesting the "right" brand, they can win a prize. The purpose here is to generate awareness and support of the brand at the retail level; these kinds of programs are especially popular in industries where consumers rely on the sales force for assistance, such as the wine or the computer software business.

Although contests can be very useful in motivating sales forces to achieve higher results, the rest of this chapter will focus on the area of consumer contests and sweepstakes. Other trade promotions are covered in Chapter 13.

Types of Sweepstakes and Contests

A contest is generally defined as an event that invites the consumer to apply skill to solve or complete a specified problem, such as finish a sentence on why they like the product, add a final line to a jingle, write a limerick, or name a product or trade character. The structure is limited only by the marketer's imagination and goals.

In a contest, entrants may be required to provide a proof of purchase or other consideration to enter, or they may have to satisfy some prerequisite in order to have their entries judged.

Winners of sweepstakes, on the other hand, are determined on the basis of chance. No skill or knowledge is necessary. Although a sponsor may suggest a proof of purchase or other form of entry eligibility, it cannot be required, since doing so would transform the sweepstakes into a lottery, which for-profit organizations may not conduct in the United States.

Sweepstakes are run in several ways. In the simplest type, consumers submit entry forms and the winner is chosen at random from all those submitted. Another type assigns numbers to consumers and selects the winning number in advance; usually, however, entrants must submit their numbers back to the company in order to be eligible. "Instant win" sweepstakes allow consumers to scratch off, peel off, or otherwise remove a covering on a game piece to find out if they have won a prize. (In some such "instant win" games, consumers may get the prize only if they correctly complete some exercise, such as answering a trivia question, and then scratch off the appropriate section of the ticket.) Other sweepstakes may give consumers game pieces that include entry numbers or symbols; individuals must then visit a specific retailer, watch a

Exhibit 8.4 An Instant-Win Sweepstakes

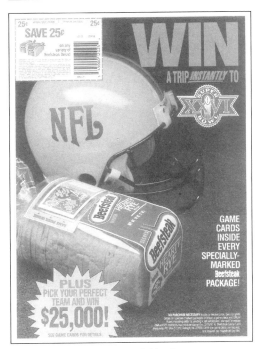

Source: Courtesy of Continental Baking Company.

particular television show, or take some other action to find out if they have won a prize. Finally, some sweepstakes now allow consumers to enter electronically, either by calling a toll-free number or by communicating with the company via computer modem.

Uses of Sweepstakes and Contests

The use of sweepstakes and contests by marketers has become somewhat more frequent during recent years. The renewed interest in this form of sales promotion activity can be attributed to a number of factors:

- Sweepstakes and contests can create consumer interest and excitement. This is especially important considering that many individuals—especially young people—have become relatively indifferent to advertising and other conventional means of promoting products.

Exhibit 8.5   A High-Involvement Consumer Sweepstakes

Source: Courtesy of Red Baron Pizza.

- As advertising costs have increased, the amount of money companies must spend on contest or sweepstakes prizes has begun to seem like more of a bargain. This can be especially true when a joint promotion can be developed with manufacturers of relatively high-priced goods (such as computers or furniture) who provide prizes at cost, or free, in exchange for the publicity value.

- Sweepstakes and, especially, contests may attract free media attention, both while the search is taking place and after winners are announced.

- Conducting sweepstakes or contests can provide a good way for a company to collect information about its consumers for its customer database. Consumers entering such promotions may be required to provide their names and addresses, and may also be persuaded to answer other questions about themselves.

- New forms of technology have made it easier for companies running some kinds of contests, such as those conducted using interactive technology, to screen for multiple sweepstakes entries. This makes it less likely that "professional entrants" will always win.

In order to be successful, sweepstakes and contests should be designed to meet particular marketing goals. For instance, many sweepstakes are designed to bring consumers closer to purchasing the product through the act of entering the event. When McDonald's runs its "instant win" sweepstakes (such as its successful Monopoly promotion), consumers must stop by one of its outlets to pick up a game piece. The idea here is that, once in a restaurant, consumers will decide to make a purchase—and, in fact, these promotions have been successful both in improving store traffic and in increasing sales. Similarly, in magazine sales sweepstakes, consumers must mail in their order forms to Publishers Clearing House or American Family Publishers to be eligible for sweepstakes prizes; since they are mailing in the entry form anyway, many will go ahead and order a magazine.

An even more direct way of attempting to get sweepstakes entrants to buy the product is to make it extremely difficult to enter if no purchase is made. For instance, Publishers Clearing House has required entrants to hunt through materials to find entry stickers making them eligible to win different prizes; purchasing a magazine, on the other hand, enters the consumer in all the contests automatically. Some organizations also threaten to remove consumers from mailing lists for future contests if they do not buy a product when they enter the sweepstakes. Although theoretically consumers can write to the company and request an entry form, most realize they are not going to go to the trouble of doing that, and therefore may be slightly more likely to make a purchase in order to stay on the list.

Despite the fact that sweepstakes and contests can sometimes persuade consumers to make a purchase, however, their main benefit seems to be at creating awareness of—and positive feeling

Exhibit 8.6   A Sweepstakes Prompting Retailer Visits

Source: Courtesy of Sara Lee Knit Products.

toward—the brand. The game-like element of these promotions seems to make them especially popular among children and young adults, who often express boredom with advertising or other types of product promotions.

In order to maximize the brand-enhancing potential of sweepstakes or contests, however, they should be planned carefully. Promotions designed to reinforce the product's name or positive attributes may be especially beneficial. Mitsubishi, for instance, reinforced the brand name of its Eclipse automobile by running a sweepstakes centered around an eclipse of the sun. ReNu contact-lens solution emphasized its quality and concern for its consumers' vision through a promotion giving away free eye exams to hundreds of consumers.

Exhibit 8.7   Sweepstakes Reinforcing Brand Benefits

Source: Courtesy of Bausch & Lomb, Inc.

In addition, sweepstakes and contests, especially those targeted at young people, must be carefully developed if they are to capture consumers' attention effectively. Picking up on consumer trends or understanding what kinds of challenges are likely to interest them can often make such promotions more successful. For example, after discovering that youngsters had started to emulate a scream that appeared in one of the commercials for its videogames, Sega sponsored an online contest that allowed consumers to compare their own version of the scream to the company president's. Procter & Gamble's Sunny Delight juice beverage, on the other hand, inadvertently created a particularly successful promotion when they scattered images of "SunnyD" in sites throughout the Internet. Although the game was intended to be a scavenger hunt with hints leading consumers from one site to the next, many enterprising young computer hackers—who tend to be heavy consumers of soft drinks and are relatively indifferent to most product promotions—began competing with one another to create the fastest search engine to locate the bottles without resorting to using the clues.

Prizes

The prizes and prize structures of contests and sweepstakes obviously have much to do with their success or failure. One popular prize structure is a pyramid consisting of a major grand prize of large value, a series of smaller prizes of intermediate value, and a large number of prizes of small or token value (such as samples of the product). However, many companies have recently noted that consumers look more at the value of the prize than at their chance of winning, and therefore companies may sacrifice secondary prizes in order to have a more attractive grand prize.

To make a sweepstakes or contest successful, it is important to choose a prize that appeals to the target audience. Cash tends to have the broadest appeal, and it is the most appropriate prize for targeting a mass audience. (Large cash prizes also have the advantage of allowing companies the opportunity to spread out payment over a large number of years; few companies announce loudly that the $10 million or whatever they're giving away may be worth much less if calculated at the present value of money.)

Although cash is the most frequently used and the most appealing prize, in some cases other prizes, or a selection of prizes, may have even more appeal, particularly if those prizes are difficult to purchase in the marketplace. For instance, teenagers may be excited about the opportunity to meet a movie star, and readers of *Gourmet* magazine may be attracted to the opportunity to attend classes at a top cooking school in Paris. Also, forcing consumers to select prizes they want may cause them to think more seriously about the possibility that they might win something, thereby increasing the likelihood that they will remember to enter.

Exhibit 8.8   A Prize That Can't Be Bought

Source: Courtesy of Smith-Kline Beecham.

Exhibit 8.9   A Sweepstakes with Multiple Prizes

Source: Courtesy of Mars, Inc.

Costs

Developing and conducting a sweepstakes or contest involves a number of costs:

- Cost of the prizes.

- Cost of the media used to promote the event.

- Cost of entry blanks, point-of-purchase materials, and support activities at both the consumer and trade levels.

- Cost of judging entries and notifying winners. (Several organizations do this on a fee basis. The more requirements in the promotion, the greater the judging fee.)

- Incidental costs, such as legal fees and insurance.

Legal Restrictions

Legal restrictions on sweepstakes and contests are complex and may include many state and local regulations. Qualified legal counsel should always be used in developing a contest or sweepstakes to prevent problems from arising. The use of a professional contest developer may also be helpful in simplifying the many details and problems associated with creating a successful contest.

One of the major factors in ensuring the success of this kind of promotion is in having easy-to-understand rules. These will probably include most of the following:

- Clear descriptions of how prizes will be awarded.

- Qualification of entrants. The sponsor of a sweepstakes or contest may limit the requirements for participation, as long as all within a classification are eligible. (For instance, an automobile company can confine its promotion to all licensed drivers; a cigarette company might want to confine its promotions to entrants over 21 years of age. To remove any suspicion of favoritism on the part of sponsors, members of the sponsoring company and its advertising or promotion agencies are almost invariably barred from eligibility.)

- Detailed description of entry requirements (for instance: "Mail entry with bottom panel from carton of Product A or with $3'' \times 5''$ sheet of paper on which you have printed the words 'Product A' in plain block letters").

- Frequency of entry (for instance: "Only one entry per person" or "Enter as often as you like").

- Information on entry cutoff dates, date of drawing, and winners' notification dates. (Two to three months is the usual length of most contests or sweepstakes; this period gives sufficient time for proper marketing promotion and gives more entrants a chance to participate.)

- Legal protection statement. To protect the sponsor from legal complications, the rules usually state "Void where prohibited by law." In cases of sweepstakes, "No purchase required" must be included in the rules.

- Listing of prizes to be given away. In sweepstakes where prize numbers are selected in advance and must be resubmitted to be eligible, it is also important to state what will happen to prizes if winning numbers are not submitted.

- The name of the judging organization and the fact that its decision is final.

- Statement that all entries become the property of the sponsoring organization.

- Statement of situations under which the event may be canceled by the manufacturer. (This has become an especially significant issue following a problem that Kraft had with an instant-win contest, where due to a printer's mistake hundreds of purchasers "won" a van that had been intended as a single grand prize.)

Strategic Uses of Sweepstakes and Contests

Because sweepstakes and contests can attract attention and create excitement about a brand, they may sometimes succeed in creating long-term value. Like most promotions, however, sweepstakes and contests work better with certain kinds of consumers and in achieving certain kinds of goals.

Loyal Users

Because sweepstakes increase excitement and sometimes convey a product message or benefit, they may be of moderate help in reinforcing sales from current customers.

Certain types of sweepstakes may be successful at obtaining extra sales from current customers. For instance, the McDonald's sweepstakes mentioned earlier may have achieved the goal of getting occasional McDonald's customers to visit the restaurant more often in order to pick up game pieces. However, this outcome is likely to result only in situations where entry in the sweepstakes is very closely connected to purchase behavior.

Some sweepstakes and contests tie two different products together, perhaps to give a lift to the less popular one. Although this linkage can result in increased consumer awareness of the secondary product, it is debatable whether any additional sales will result.

Competitive Loyals

Although competitive loyals may enter a sweepstakes for a product they do not currently buy, they will less frequently purchase that product. It is only with competitive loyals who buy solely out of inertia that sweepstakes may have any effect, since they may cause an otherwise uninterested person to notice a particular brand. For instance, in some direct-mail sweepstakes, consumers must read promotional materials to enter; if the information is persuasive, they may consider making a purchase.

Competitive loyals entering a contest may be forced to buy the product; in some cases, the trial obtained through this purchase may prompt them to purchase it again in the future.

Switchers

Again, sweepstakes are likely to be successful in getting switchers to consider buying a brand only if the entry removes some of the obstacles that would usually cause these consumers to purchase another brand. For instance, a consumer who has to stop at a grocery store to pick up a contest entry form may also buy some groceries there, rather than making an additional stop at another store.

Consumers who switch brands for reasons of value or variety may sometimes be influenced by sweepstakes promotions because, like advertising, they offer a reminder to buy a specific brand.

Although contests may cause switchers to purchase a certain product, those consumers are unlikely to continue to do so more frequently in the future.

Price Buyers

For consumers who buy solely on the basis of price, sweepstakes may not be effective at prompting purchase. Most consumers understand that they need not make a purchase in order to enter a sweepstakes, so they are likely to continue to buy the least expensive brand on the market even if they participate in a sweepstakes promotion.

Like other types of consumers, price buyers may occasionally purchase a product in order to enter a contest, if the prize is very attractive and they believe they have a chance of winning. However, they should not be expected to continue to buy the product in the future unless the brand has strong benefits of which they were previously unaware.

Exhibit 8.10   A Contest Encouraging Increased Product Usage

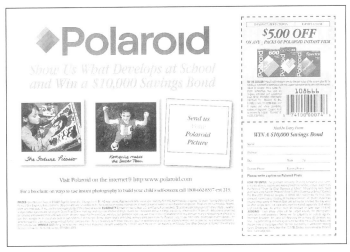

Source: Courtesy of Polaroid Corp.

Nonusers

Occasionally, a sweepstakes or contest may bring a product to the attention of nonusers of the category, and they may end up buying the product. For instance, a woman who does not currently subscribe to any magazine may obtain a Publishers Clearing House mailing and, while glancing through the sweepstakes materials, see a description of a publication she might like and order it. However, this probably happens relatively infrequently; what may occur more often is that such consumers enter the sweepstakes without buying any product.

Contests may force nonusers of a category to buy a product at least once, although they are less likely to do so in the future.

Sweepstakes and Contests and Residual Value

Sweepstakes and contests may generate some long-term value in that they may attract attention to brands and may sometimes increase positive feelings among consumers. In addition, a well-chosen prize may sometimes improve the image of the company (for instance, a sweepstakes with a top prize of tickets to Wimbledon offered by a tennis magazine might reinforce the publication's positioning as an expert in the field of tennis).

Sweepstakes and contests may sometimes increase consumers' propensity to buy a product in the future. As they tend to increase awareness rather than stimulate trial or purchase, they have more in common with advertising and public relations than with other sales promotion tactics. They are therefore often reserved for specific situations where they can be used to encourage immediate purchases, such as in the cases of mail-order or retail companies.

Because purchase can be a requirement for entering, contests may be more effective at generating product trial than sweepstakes are, and may sometimes influence consumers' long-term propensity to buy a particular product. However, as mentioned, many contests tend to have a somewhat limited appeal and relatively low response rates, so the number of people that become long-term customers as a result of a contest may be relatively small.

Exhibit 8.11   A Sweepstakes Designed to Increase Brand Value

Source: Courtesy of McCain Citrus, Inc.

CHAPTER NINE

Through-the-Mail Premiums

Through-the-mail premiums offer consumers some kind of non-monetary incentive to purchase a particular brand. Merchandise offered through these kinds of programs can be quite diverse: for example, while many premiums (such as T-shirts, glasses, or coffee mugs) are designed to reinforce the brand's name or logo, others are designed to subtly emphasize brand benefits or to capitalize on trends that may be attractive to targeted consumers of the product category.

Through-the-mail premiums are traditionally divided into two types. Free through-the-mail premiums are items offered without charge to consumers in exchange for a certain number of proofs of purchase and, perhaps, a small handling charge. Self-liquidators are items that consumers must pay to receive; the money received covers the cost of the product, meaning that the promotion is an inexpensive one for companies to run.

A hybrid through-the-mail premium plan combines both of these techniques into a "speed plan," which offers merchandise to consumers in exchange for a few proofs of purchase plus a relatively small fee. This kind of program can allow more attractive merchandise to be offered without forcing consumers to collect many proofs of purchase before they can acquire the premium.

The use of through-the-mail premiums by marketers has declined in recent years—for example, only 56 percent of pack-

Exhibit 9.1   A Free Through-the-Mail Premium

A new reason
to feel the
comfort of
the world's
#1 contact lens.

Source: Courtesy of Johnson & Johnson.

aged-goods companies reported recently using this form of sales promotion in 1995, compared to 70 percent in 1990. A primary reason for this decrease is that—although they are often attractive only to small groups of consumers and don't usually have a large impact on sales of the product—premiums are generally time-consuming to administer. In addition, since it can be hard to predict demand for the premium being offered, this kind of promotion can also be quite risky. Many marketers have offered premiums and then been saddled with leftover merchandise at the end of the promotional period, or irritated consumers by not having enough goods in stock.

Exhibit 9.2   A Premium Designed to Create Excitement
about a Parity Product

Source: Courtesy of Van den Bergh Foods Company.

Nevertheless, through-the-mail premiums have advantages that make them appropriate for certain marketing situations. Premiums often provide a good way to create attention for—and excitement about—a particular product, especially when the item being offered is especially attractive. Premiums can also be effective at reinforcing brand image and usage habits, and they may in some cases succeed in persuading consumers to buy additional product or to switch from one brand to another. Finally, they may make consumers feel good about the brand, thereby providing long-term benefits to the company offering them.

Exhibit 9.3   A Premium Reinforcing Product Advertising

Source: Courtesy of Del Monte Foods.

Uses of Premium Offers

Premium offers can be an effective way to get attention from a specific group of consumers for a brand that might otherwise appear to be at parity with other products in the category. For example, if a brand is designed to appeal to a certain group of consumers, such as teenagers, then a special premium targeted specifically at that group may successfully persuade them to try the product, or to purchase it on a more regular basis in order to obtain this premium.

Free or self-liquidating premiums may successfully provide reminders of the product, reinforcing the brand message, or helping consumers find more uses for a particular product. For example, people who own a Keebler "Hollow Tree" cookie jar are more frequently reminded of that brand. Therefore, they may be more likely to buy Keebler products in the cookie aisle and to consume them at home. Similarly, consumers who have obtained Pillsbury's booklet of pizza recipes may be tempted to use the company's refrigerated pizza dough more frequently.

Exhibit 9.4   A Premium Serving as Reminder Advertising

Source: Courtesy of The Pillsbury Company.

Premium offers can also be helpful in rewarding and, in some cases, increasing the immediate consumption of a product by current users. For instance, the offer of a free T-shirt may be perceived as a desirable incentive by users of a particular product, and those people may increase their purchases or buy a larger product package in order to obtain the premium.

Premium offers are usually relatively easy to set up and may be fairly inexpensive compared with other types of sales promotions. For example, provided that enough consumers order the premium, the only costs associated with self-liquidators are the advertising and administrative; if the premium is priced above the manufacturer's cost, the promotion may provide a profit to the organization even if sales of the product do not increase. Through-the-mail premiums offered free to consumers in exchange for purchases of the product are less likely to be profitable, although the increase in consumer interest in the product and consumer slippage (additional purchases from people who neglect to actually send in for the refund) may make this type of promotion immediately worthwhile.

Finally, premium offers can be an effective means of obtaining names and addresses of consumers who have purchased the product. Marketers who are considering implementing or extending database marketing programs in the future can use this information.

The main problem with through-the-mail promotions is that they are often not effective in increasing sales of the product. Most consumers will either have no interest in the premium or will not be willing to collect proofs of purchase or pay money to get it. Offering through-the-mail premiums may also be risky for marketers. If the program doesn't go as well as planned, the company may be stuck with the leftover merchandise.

Because premiums are difficult to test, most marketing managers rely on historical experience or their own judgment when developing promotional plans and estimating demand. However, the following suggestions and guidelines may be useful.

Developing Premium Offers

Premium Selection

As mentioned earlier, some of the best premiums reinforce the brand name or benefits of the product being promoted, or encourage usage of the product. For instance, a soft-drink manufacturer may offer T-shirts that sport a popular advertising slogan, or the manufacturer of a cake mix may supply a decorative cake pan that is particularly attractive to children and therefore encourages more frequent cake-baking.

It is also important that premiums be perceived as desirable to the target audience for the brand, or (in certain cases) to the children or other relatives of the target. Trendy or unusual items, especially if they cannot be purchased anywhere else, often make quite successful premiums. For example, Frito-Lay, Pepsi Cola, and Hershey once ran a joint promotion that offered storybooks from the popular "Goosebumps" series that could not be obtained elsewhere. Premiums tied to special events, such as the Olympics, also may be effective. And in recent years, several companies have successfully offered premiums consisting of items that many consumers use on an ongoing basis, such as free long-distance telephone minutes or miles in a frequent-flyer program.

Another type of premium that has become particularly popu-

Exhibit 9.5   A Premium of Long-Distance Telephone Time

Source: Courtesy of Golden Valley Microwave Foods, Inc.

lar in recent years is the company-sponsored magazine. These magazines generally provide articles as well as advertising copy that are of particular interest to the target for the product. For example, *Nintendo Power* offers strategies and product previews for videogame players, *Guess Journal* and Benetton's *Colors* provide fashion information, *Disney* appeals to young people, and Marlboro's *Unlimited* provides general-interest articles for young men. While some of these publications are provided free to consumers upon request, others (such as *Nintendo Power*) have become pop-

Exhibit 9.6   A High-Value Premium

Source: Courtesy of Uncle Ben's, Inc.

ular enough that millions of people have been willing to pay for a subscription.

For premium promotions to be successful, it is important that the items being offered are perceived as desirable, and that they appeal to the appropriate consumer target. Unusual items that cannot be purchased anywhere else are often quite successful, as are items that are less expensive through the promotion than they might be in a retail store.

Although the total value of most premiums is fairly small (for instance, no more than $10 or $20), some marketers have had very good experiences with self-liquidators that require the consumer to pay hundreds or even thousands of dollars to obtain them. Consumers who are used to buying from catalogs may be the most attracted to this kind of promotion. The offer of brand name merchandise and of an unconditional guarantee of a refund if the product is not what was expected can also be helpful in making consumers willing to invest in such an expensive item.

Delivery

It is generally very important that through-the-mail premiums be delivered promptly, or at least by the date promised on the order

Exhibit 9.7 A Premium Offered Through an FSI

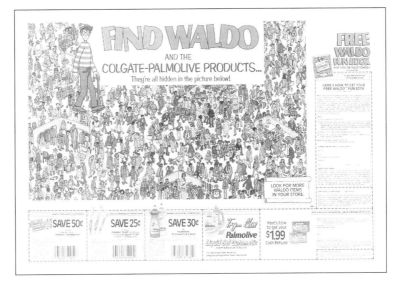

Source: Courtesy of Colgate-Palmolive Company.

form. This is especially critical in the case of self-liquidators, where consumers have paid money to obtain the premium. If consumers (who in some cases may have ordered the premium for a specific usage occasion or to give as a gift) do not receive the item in a timely fashion, they are likely to be annoyed, and any goodwill generated by the promotion may be lost. If an unexpected delay is experienced (if, for example, demand is larger than expected and additional product must be produced), consumers should be informed of this fact with an apologetic note, and they should be allowed to cancel their orders or (if feasible) choose another item instead.

It is also important that premiums reach the consumer in good condition. Merchandise shipped should include a phone number that can be used to contact the company in the event that merchandise arrives broken or with other problems.

Costs

An important issue in the development of premium programs is determining how much to charge or how many proofs of purchase to require in exchange for the item being offered. Most manufacturers choose levels that make the promotion attractive and—for self-liquidators—result in a small profit or a not-too-large loss. The goal is to create consumer goodwill and reinforce the product name and benefits rather than to make a great deal of money. Even programs that are entirely self-liquidating often require consumers to send in at least one or a few proofs of purchase from the product. This may reinforce the idea that the premium is tied to the brand and may also help to generate a few immediate sales.

In addition to the cost of the premium, there are other costs associated with this type of promotion technique:

1. Postage to return the premium. Often this is charged to the consumer as a handling fee. If it is not, it is a cost to the advertiser.

2. Packing and handling the premium. This includes the fees of the redemption facility that takes care of the orders and the materials necessary to ship the premium to the consumer.

3. Any promotional material to be used in the store or returned with the premium, such as a "bounce-back" coupon offer.

Experience shows that it is usually best to pay a fulfillment house to handle the orders and shipping of premiums. Unless an organization has the people and equipment necessary to handle fulfillment properly, it can present a great many problems in terms of time and money.

Promotional Methods

While some premium offers may be effectively promoted on the product packaging, advertising the promotion through a free-standing newspaper insert (FSI) or in other media is likely to produce a larger number of immediate sales. Another way to promote a premium offer is at the point of purchase, but, since most through-the-mail premium offers do not result in strong sales gains, retailers may be reluctant to promote these offers in the store.

However premiums are advertised, it is important to give complete specifications about the item being offered. Sizes, colors, and other details should be supplied in order to help consumers visualize what they are ordering.

The Offer and the Return Coupon

Unfortunately, one of the major problems with premiums is that sometimes the marketer makes it difficult for the consumer to understand the offer and even more difficult to obtain the premium. Therefore the offer should be made as clearly and as simply as possible. When practical, it is helpful to show an example of the proof of purchase required and to explain how to remove it. It should also be as easy as possible for consumers to meet the requirements set for redemption.

One of the biggest problems can be the coupon order blank. The blank should include all information needed to fill the order, including enough room for consumers to supply the required information and spaces for the zip code and other pertinent data.

Response

Although a traditional method of evaluating the success of premium offers is to look at the number of orders filled, this is not usually an appropriate measure of this sales promotion technique. Objectives set for the sales promotion program in the planning stage, not the number of premiums redeemed, should be the basis for evaluation. No one should really care how many premiums are moved except the premium supplier.

It is important for manufacturers to accurately predict the response rate for a premium offer, however, so that an appropriate number of items may be ordered. As a general guide, self-liquidating and free through-the-mail premiums usually don't achieve orders above 1 percent of the gross circulation of the advertising media where the offer appears. For example, if the offer is made in FSIs with a total combined circulation of 2,000,000 copies, then returns from the premium would be expected to be around 20,000. Of course, some offers run well ahead of that estimate and some well below it, depending on the premium itself, the price of the product, and the value of the offer.

Strategic Uses of Premium Offers

Although premiums do not usually have a great immediate impact on sales, they may nevertheless be effective. They can help marketers achieve specific goals with certain kinds of consumers,

Exhibit 9.8   A Premium Targeted at Current Users

Source: Courtesy of Heinz Pet Products.

including attracting interest, reinforcing brand message, and encouraging increased usage.

Loyal Users

Consumers who currently use a particular brand are often attracted to premiums offered in connection with that product. For example, since these consumers already have positive feelings about the brand, they may be more likely to want a T-shirt or a coffee mug bearing the brand name. Also, because these people are buying the product anyway, they may be more willing to collect the proofs of purchase needed to get the premium.

Exhibit 9.9 A Premium Encouraging Increased
Product Usage

Source: Courtesy of McCormick & Company, Inc.

After the premium is received, it may remind consumers of the product, thereby promoting further brand loyalty. Finally, consumers who feel they are getting a "reward" for purchasing the product may feel more positive about the brand in the future. This dynamic may be different than the one that occurs with other sales promotion tactics such as couponing, where consumers may begin to believe that the discounted price is the "real" price of the product and therefore may be unwilling to pay more for it.

Premiums in some cases may encourage consumers to load up on the product or use it more frequently. For instance, a manufacturer of Chinese grocery products might encourage purchase and usage of its soy sauce and water chestnuts by offering consumers a wok or a simplified Chinese cookbook as a premium.

Competitive Loyals

People who use another brand on a regular basis are unlikely to want an item that features the name of a brand they don't use, and so they are likely to be poor targets for many premiums that serve as reminders of a particular brand. They are also unlikely to purchase a product very many times in order to receive a free-in-the-mail premium.

A self-liquidating premium may, infrequently, be very attractive to the user of a competitive product. When this does happen, the consumer may buy the product to get the required proof of purchase, and trial may be achieved. However, whether this trial converts the consumer into a future buyer depends on a number of factors, such as the quality of the product, previous experience (or lack thereof) with the brand, and the strength of the loyalty to the product currently being used.

Switchers

Switchers may often take advantage of self-liquidating or free-in-the-mail premium offers, although they probably are somewhat less likely to do so than are current loyal users. The strategic benefits of using premiums to attract switchers are basically the same as those achieved with loyal users—possible increased purchases in order to obtain the product, reinforced brand message or increased usage, and goodwill toward the company providing the premium.

Price Buyers

Price buyers may in many cases be attracted to premium offers (especially those that offer merchandise free in the mail or that give a good deal on something they wanted to acquire anyway). However, it is rare that this type of promotion will cause this consumer type to purchase the product beyond what is necessary to obtain the required proofs of purchase to get the premium.

Nonusers

Like competitive loyals, nonusers of a product category are fairly unlikely to be interested in most premiums offered by brands in the category, and they probably will infrequently notice promotional materials for those premiums. Only in the case of a self-liquidating premium (advertised through mass media) that is particularly attractive and a very good deal might they be willing to participate. Although this unlikely scenario may cause these consumers to purchase and try the product, they usually will not continue to do so in the future, unless the product has "hidden" benefits or is markedly better than the others in the category that the nonuser might have tried in the past.

Through-the-Mail Premiums and Residual Value

Perhaps the primary reason for manufacturers to offer through-the-mail premiums is the residual value that these types of promotions generate. Although most premiums do not generate a large amount of immediate volume, their continued use in the future can often cause consumers to remember the product better and, possibly, to use more of it. Through-the-mail premiums can also be good attention-getters and may promote good feelings about the brand among consumers, increasing the likelihood of obtaining future sales.

CHAPTER TEN

Sampling Programs

S ampling is one sure method of putting a product directly into the consumer's hands. Most other sales promotion techniques require consumers to take a chance by spending their own money in order to be able to use the product. Sampling, however, allows consumers to try a product with no financial risk. In addition, samples may be perceived as a gift from the manufacturer by some consumers, and therefore may generate considerable goodwill. As a result, sampling is one of the most popular forms of sales promotion. For example, Donnelley Marketing reported that marketers spent about 10 percent of their consumer promotion budgets on sampling in 1994.

The one disadvantage of sampling is that it tends to be expensive. Since the product is given free to consumers, up-front costs of sampling programs tend to be high. Nevertheless, the high trial rate and the frequently excellent conversion rate (the number of triers who become buyers) of sampling programs often make them worthwhile.

As effective as sampling is, however, it won't work for all products. Sampling is most successful when the brand has a demonstrable point of difference or advantage over the competition—that is, when trying the product demonstrates that it is better, more effective, or more efficient. Sampling also works very well for products that can't really be described in advertising and that need to be used or demonstrated for the benefit to be appreciated. On the other hand, sampling is particularly costly for products that are highly specialized or appeal only to small, select markets, such as rug hookers or antique collectors, since these people may be hard to find and since sampling to a broader audience may result in a large amount of waste. Products that appeal to narrow groups that cannot be easily reached should be sampled only if they have important benefits that can be readily observed through trial.

Sampling is frequently used to stimulate trial of a new or improved product, to encourage new uses for an established brand, or to call attention to a new package. Sampling can be a good way to build or broaden sales of an established brand in fringe or new geographic areas. It also can be used to encourage trial in a new consumer category or through new distribution outlets, or to introduce consumers just entering the category to the product (such as new mothers to Pampers or 13-year-olds to Clearasil).

Methods of Sampling

Like couponing, sampling is distinguished by the distribution methods used to place the samples in the hands of prospects. As a general rule, the more directly the product is put into the hands of consumers, the more costly it is. Sampling distribution techniques are often limited or dictated by the product itself. If the product is bulky, a through-the-mail sampling plan is probably out. If it is perishable, in-packs or on-packs can't be used.

Direct Mail

In direct-mail sampling, the sample is sent directly to prospects via the U.S. Postal Service. The major problems here are limitations on what can be mailed or shipped, as well as the expense. Direct-mail delivery is not usually appropriate for products that are perishable, bulky, or heavy, for example. In addition, mailing even small samples can be expensive, since the Postal Service charges by the ounce for handling them.

Despite these limitations, however, direct mail is an excellent method of sampling, often three to four times more effective than couponing at getting consumers to purchase the product in the future. Depending on the marketing goals for the product, direct mail can deliver samples to precisely targeted groups of consumers or to almost every household in the United States. Trial often reaches 70 to 80 percent of the homes sampled.

Exhibit 10.1   A Direct-Mail Sample

Source: Courtesy of General Mills, Inc.

Door-to-Door

In door-to-door sampling, the product is personally delivered to consumers' homes, usually by an independent delivery or sampling service. The person making the delivery either leaves the sample on the doorstep (or hanging on the doorknob) or delivers it to the person answering the door. (It is illegal to place samples delivered by alternatives to the Postal Service in any U.S. mailbox.)

Exhibit 10.2   A Sample Delivered Door-to-Door

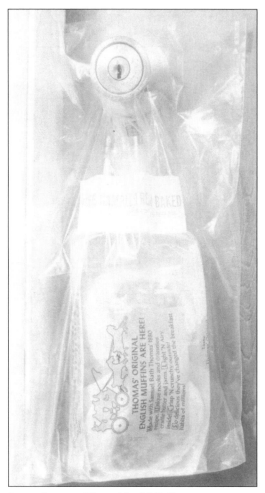

Source: Courtesy of Thomas' English Muffins.

Door-to-door sampling has the advantage of being able to deliver more bulky or semi-perishable samples, but it does have some disadvantages. For one thing, the only targeting that generally can be done is by geographic area, since alternative delivery is usually cost-effective only if samples are dropped at every home in a particular neighborhood. In addition, this type of sampling is usually appropriate only for certain fairly dense suburban or urban neighborhoods where individuals live in detached or semi-detached homes. Other types of neighborhoods may present specific prob-

Exhibit 10.3   A Central Location Demonstration

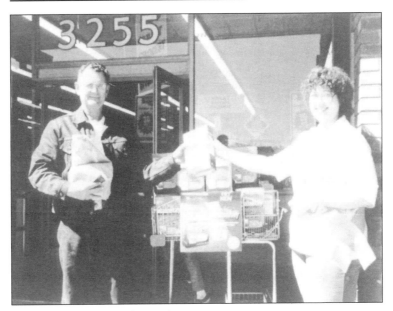

Source: Courtesy of Stratmar Systems, Inc.

lems: delivery costs may be too expensive in rural areas, while the samples may not reach their intended targets if left in apartment buildings or certain urban areas where they may be stolen. Another problem is that door-to-door sampling has been outlawed in some communities.

Central Location/Demonstrator

Another popular method of putting the product into prospects' hands—and one that may stimulate high consumer involvement— is central-location sampling by demonstrators. The product may be given to prospects in a store, at a shopping mall, on a street corner, at a transportation terminal or in some other public building. In some cases, prospects are given a sample of the product to use later; in other cases, consumers may try the product then and there, perhaps with help from a demonstrator. For example, in a supermarket Pepsi may be compared to Coke or bite-sized pieces of a new sausage may be cooked and distributed on toothpicks. In a department store makeup may be applied to the consumer's skin or a food processor may be demonstrated.

Demonstrator sampling may be especially appropriate for products that require preparation (such as food products that need to be cooked) or perishable items (such as ice cream). In addition, products with benefits that can be appreciated only through a demonstration, or involve a risk of some sort, are often promoted with this kind of sampling program. For example, a test drive is standard for consumers considering purchasing automobiles, which are expensive and difficult to judge without trial. On a more pedestrian level, sampling of foods that appeal to children is popular in grocery stores, since many parents do not want to risk buying new foods that their children might not want to eat.

In-store sampling has become increasingly important in recent years, mostly because most shopping decisions today are made when consumers are actually in the store. Marketers spent about $125 million on supermarket sampling and demonstrations in 1995, up 15 percent from the year before. One problem, however, is that some supermarkets do not permit sampling, or limit the number of vendors allowed to participate, saying that such programs tend to be messy and hinder store traffic flow on busy shopping days. Many other retailers, however, have found that consumers seem to enjoy the opportunity to try a variety of products before purchasing, and therefore are willing to tolerate the disadvantages of sampling demonstrators in order to foster customer goodwill.

Co-Op or Selective

Market-service groups have organized distribution methods to reach selective population subgroups, such as brides, the military, college students, or new mothers, with a package of noncompeting products that have special appeal to them. For instance, college students may receive a "survival kit" with aspirin, shampoo, and No-Doz upon arriving at school. The major advantage here is the ability to reach targeted groups that might otherwise be difficult to sample efficiently.

Products may also be sampled selectively to people who are traveling or attending some kind of event. For example, manufacturers may provide guest-sized soaps and toiletries to hotels in the hope that people who try them on the road will then purchase them to use at home. Airline meals are another popular way to introduce an upscale, captive audience to products: for example, Anheuser-Busch introduced its Eagle honey-roasted peanuts to airline passengers before selling them in stores, and United Airlines agreed to serve Starbucks coffee on all its flights. Other compa-

Exhibit 10.4   Sample Distributed Through Co-Op Mailing

Source: Courtesy of S. C. Johnson & Son.

nies selling products such as wines or soft drinks may successfully achieve trial by making them available free to consumers attending fund-raisers, concerts, or sporting events.

Newspapers and Magazines

Relatively few products can be sampled effectively through newspapers and magazines, though there are some exceptions. The major limitation of this method of distribution is that it can work only for products small and thin enough to be bound or inserted into the publication. One example of a product promoted effectively through these media are the perfume samples often inserted into magazines; newer twists on this idea allow consumers to sam-

Exhibit 10.5   An Advertisement for Magazine Lipstick Sampling Technology

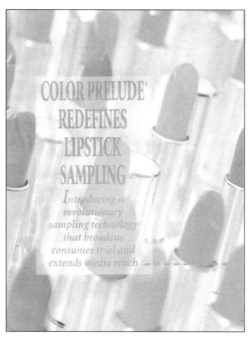 

Source: Courtesy of Color Prelude.

ple the aromas of such products as the leather in a Rolls-Royce or ultra-premium cigarettes made by R.J. Reynolds. Other products such as lipsticks, hair-care products, stationery, or fabric samples may also be appropriately sampled through this method.

Sample Packages in Stores

Another important method of sampling is the sale of trial-sized packages in retail stores. Miniatures of products are manufactured and sold to retailers, who then sell the samples to consumers. This is an effective way to get trial at very low cost—in fact, both the manufacturer and the retailer may realize a profit on the sales of these trial-sized products. Retailers may especially like this sampling method because it gives them margin on samples that might otherwise be given away free.

Another version of this tactic combines several trial-sized items in a product line into one item, which is often sold at a premium price. For instance, Kraft encouraged trial of its new non-cheddar Cracker Barrel varieties with a "sampler" that included five

Exhibit 10.6   Sampling of a Product Sent Through an FSI

Source: Courtesy of Reckitt & Colman, Inc.

1-ounce flavors of cheese for a relatively low price. The sampler itself appealed to certain kinds of snackers, and it also prompted trial of the new flavors that consumers might have otherwise ignored.

Exhibit 10.7   Coupon for Free Trial Size

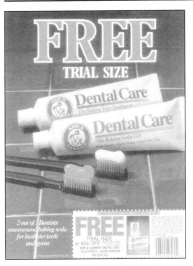

Source: Courtesy of Church & Dwight Co., Inc.

Exhibit 10.8   A Coupon for a Free Sample

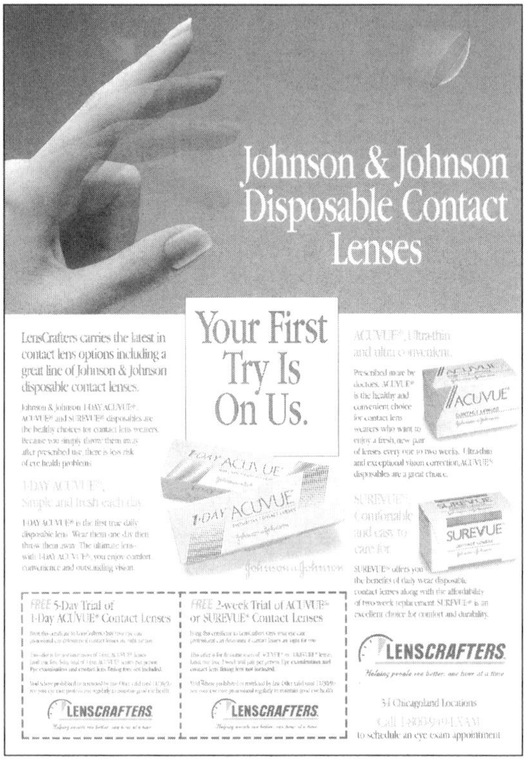

Source: Courtesy of Johnson & Johnson and LensCrafters.

Coupons for Free Samples

Sometimes manufacturers distribute to consumers coupons that can be exchanged for regular-size containers of the product in a retail outlet. This method of sampling is preferable for products that require extensive testing by consumers before benefits become obvious. In addition, this tactic may be more efficient than others because only consumers who are interested in the product are likely to make the effort to find the product in the store. (A disadvantage, however, is that those consumers who never use coupons will be missed.) Finally, although it can be somewhat expensive to offer a full-size container of a product to consumers, and although coupons are subject to handling charges (and may be redeemed fraudulently), elimination of the high delivery costs of other methods of sample distribution may make this one worthwhile. It may be especially appropriate for products that are bulky (such as paper towels) or perishable (such as yogurt) and therefore particularly difficult to deliver in any other way.

In-Pack or On-Pack

In some cases a sample may be delivered to consumers with another product from the same manufacturer, serving as a premium. Although this technique is the least expensive way to distribute samples, it also has limited exposure since the sample is distributed only to present users of the carrying product. Usually this technique works best with brands that are somehow related to one another, such as coffee and nondairy creamer.

Exhibit 10.9   A Trade Advertisement for an On-Pack Cross-Ruff Sample

Source: Courtesy of Bic Pen Corporation.

Exhibit 10.10   Sample Available Through Consumer
Request

A message to
50 million
Americans who
can't digest
dairy foods.
Now you can.

DAIRY
EASE

For free trial call
1-800-233-7500, ext. 211.

Dairy Ease does what no antacid can. It supple-
ments the lactase your body needs to digest lac-
tose, so you can enjoy your favorite dairy foods
without discomfort. And right now, you can try
Dairy Ease *absolutely free.*

Source: Courtesy of Glenbrook Laboratories.

Consumer Request

In some cases, especially when products are expensive or used by a small percentage of the population, consumers may receive product samples only by request, usually through a mail-in or a toll-free telephone offer. This type of sample may be free or may require a small payment to defray some of the cost of the product and to demonstrate that consumers are truly serious in their interest. These offers may be publicized through any available means, including mass-media advertising, free-standing inserts, direct mail, in-store displays, in-packs or on-packs, interactive marketing sites, and public relations. For instance, through magazine ads, General Foods once offered samples of a new gourmet coffee to consumers who called a toll-free telephone number, while Ralston Purina offered samples of its gourmet O.N.E. dog food in free-standing inserts to consumers through direct response. Manufacturers of expensive perfume often offer samples through co-op offers in magazines, with a required payment of $1 or $2 for each sample ordered.

Exhibit 10.11   A Trial-Size Sample Available by Request

Source: Courtesy of Ralston Purina Company.

The advantage of this type of self-selected sampling program is that waste is eliminated. Since consumers who respond are likely to be especially good prospects, a more expensive sample can be offered. In addition, this type of program can help marketers to establish a database of consumers who are likely to be good future prospects. For example, once Ralston Purina obtained a list of dog owners through its sample offer, it would be possible to target them with information about other pet products.

Uses of Samples

As stated earlier, sampling is the most effective way to gain trial for a product, and it is particularly appropriate for products that are new or that suffer from low awareness or small market share. Unlike advertising, which usually takes time to work, sampling may quickly convince consumers to buy a particular product. In fact, in some cases, such as categories with high brand loyalty, sampling may be the *only* way to get consumers to try a new product or brand.

In addition, although the total cost of sampling programs can be high, sampling can be quite efficient at obtaining broad-based trial from a majority of the population, or at targeting specific segments. Finally, because sampling is so effective at building demand, the announcement of a major sampling program can be useful in gaining distribution for a new product and in getting in-store displays or other trade support.

The main problem with sampling programs is that they tend to be quite expensive, and therefore should be considered as long-term investments. Products sent through the mail are subject to problems in delivery, timeliness, and condition, and many methods of distribution may result in theft or pilferage.

Like all promotional programs, of course, sampling works best at building long-term brand value when the product being promoted has a definite advantage over others in the category. This should be considered when predicting the likely success of a sampling program.

Costs

It is impossible to give accurate costs of sampling programs, because they vary so widely and change so rapidly. However, methods that can be used to estimate costs of sampling programs include:

1. The cost of direct mail depends on the weight of the product and the postal charges at the time the sample is mailed. In addition to the cost of the sample, other charges that must be included are the mailing list, the carton, the addressing, the handling, the postage, and any return materials (such as coupons).

2. Door-to-door distribution costs vary widely, depending on such variables as the number of homes to be covered, how close together the homes are, the availability of a sampling organization in the community, and the regional location. Again, the cost of the product, the door hanger or other method of attaching the product to the home, and the coupons distributed must be included in the budgeted amount.

3. An in-store product demonstrator usually charges a flat rate per day, regardless of how many units are distributed. The cost of the product, sales promotion materials, and any coupons that are distributed also must be included.

4. A cooperative mailing to specialized groups is usually less expensive than many other forms of sampling. The mailing charges, the cost of the product and any sales promotion materials must be included.

5. The in-pack or on-pack method usually costs less than any other type of sampling. Since the only costs are usually for the product, the attachment or insertion, and any promotional materials, the sample can get to the consumer with little or no actual distribution costs.

As a general rule, the following costs can be incurred in the preparation or execution of a sampling program:

- The sampled product

- Direct-mail or list charges

- Postage or distribution costs

- Handling fees, such as those charged by direct-mail organizations

- Advertising or other sales promotion material costs that might be included in the sample package

- The cost of cartons, boxes, or other materials used to distribute the product

- Retailer and/or clearinghouse charges for coupons distributed with the sample, including the face value of the coupon

- Cost of insertion or attachment for in-pack or on-pack sampling

Product Selection

Some products sample better than others. For example, sampling has traditionally been used most frequently to introduce new or improved products to consumers in the hope that they will buy those brands in the future. In recent years, however, manufacturers have frequently used samples to promote established products as well as new ones. More than 70 percent of surveyed manufac-turers in 1995 reported having recently used samples to promote existing products, compared to only 43 percent in 1991.

This increase in the sampling of existing products appears to be due to the realization (made especially clear through the analy-sis of scanner data that record consumer purchases over multiple shopping trips) that many people have never purchased a number of available products in particular categories, and therefore may be persuaded to change their future buying habits through sam-pling efforts. Sampling for existing products may be especially use-ful when product proliferation in the category is high, when one or two brands in the category have high brand loyalty, or when new users frequently enter the category.

Other considerations in determining what products should be sampled are how frequently items in the category are purchased as well as the size of the potential target market. Products that are purchased infrequently are often poor prospects for sampling pro-grams because even if triers purchase the product in the future, the profit margins from the purchases may not be enough to com-pensate for the original sampling effort. In addition, mass sampling for products that are likely to be used by only a small percentage of the population is likely to be inefficient; if such products are sampled, it should be done through more targeted programs or through consumer request.

Finally, sampling is likely to be most appropriate for products that are noticeably better than the competition in some way. Prod-ucts that do not have at least a perceived competitive advantage are likely to fail anyway, of course, but sampling programs may make this occur even more quickly.

Timing

Usually sampling works best if it is done just before any seasonal upswing in sales or use of the product. This helps to generate usage and can result in extra sales.

A general rule of sampling is not to commence the program until there is sufficient retail distribution—normally at least 50 per-cent distribution in retail stores that would be expected to stock the product. Consumers who try a brand but cannot find it at the retail level may become annoyed and forget about the product.

Samples should always be large enough for consumers to get a fair trial of the product. Of course, the exact size depends on the benefit being claimed for the product. If it is something that tastes good, one serving can be enough. If it is something that requires continued use to see the benefits, then a larger size to allow multiple uses is in order.

As a general rule, a regular-size container of a product will produce more trial than a smaller sample, although distributing a regular-size sample may allow consumers to postpone purchasing the product. If a smaller size is used, it should be a miniature of the regular package so that consumers will know what the product looks like when they go to the store to buy it.

Sampling and Other Forms of Promotion

Generally, sampling should take place following the brand's establishment in retail stores and following its introduction to consumers through advertising. By the time consumers receive their samples (or see offers detailing how to get them), they should ideally already be aware of the product and, perhaps, have an interest in it.

Advertising may also be used to announce that samples are available or that they are currently being distributed, in the case of a broad-based effort. Nutra-Sweet, the manufacturer of the artificial sweetener Equal, even reminded consumers of its sampling of the product with gumballs years *after* the promotional effort, in order to reinforce positive feelings about the product and to increase brand loyalty.

Probably the most effective way to maximize the effect of sampling on sales is to include a coupon with the sample. For consumers who like the product and who use coupons, this may provide extra impetus to make that first purchase. However, this may be appropriate only for products that are purchased frequently, not for items (such as perfume) that will likely be purchased only once or occasionally in the future.

Strategic Uses of Sampling Programs

Sampling tends to be more effective than other kinds of sales promotion programs in certain kinds of situations. Although sampling may be effective at reminding certain occasional users of the existence of a particular product, it also can be successful in winning over consumers who currently use other products or even those who are nonusers of the product category.

Loyal Users

Consumers who currently are loyal to a brand will generally be unaffected by receiving a sample of the product. These people have already tried the product and like it; they need no further convincing. Sampling to these consumers may result in sharply reduced profits, since samples are expensive and may substitute for purchases that would have been made if the consumer had not received the free merchandise.

Competitive Loyals

Sampling may be very effective at winning over consumers who are current users of competitive products—in fact, sampling may be the *only* way to get many of these consumers to try or consider buying a product other than their regular brand.

In order for sampling programs to be effective with these consumers, however, the product must demonstrate some sort of noticeable superiority to the currently used brand. Advertising or promotional materials should point out this product benefit; the inclusion of a coupon with the sample can reinforce propensity to buy if the consumer reaction is positive.

Switchers

Switchers who have occasionally used a brand in the past are unlikely to be affected very much by sampling programs. Since these consumers already have experience with the product and are still not using it on a regular basis, one more experience with it is not likely to make much difference in their future propensity to buy.

There are exceptions to this, however. One might be when consumers have used a product in the past but for some reason have "forgotten" about it. For instance, Kellogg's Corn Flakes could have conceivably distributed samples of the product to complement its campaign "Taste them again for the first time," which was designed to regain former users of the product. (Whether these consumers would be considered switchers or simply competitive users is debatable, however.)

In-store sampling also may prompt infrequent users to purchase products, especially impulse items, when they otherwise would not have done so. Here, sampling seems to work well as a point-of-purchase reminder of the product, but it is, of course, even more effective than regular point-of-purchase materials because the consumer actually experiences the product.

In certain select cases sampling may also cause switchers or competitive loyals to reevaluate their allegiance (or lack thereof) to a particular brand. For example, the famous "Pepsi Challenge" was designed to convince Coke drinkers or switchers that they really did prefer Pepsi.

As previously mentioned, sampling can be a successful tool in getting distribution for a product, because retailers generally believe that it will increase consumer demand.

Price Buyers

Although price buyers may use a free sample, they are usually unlikely to buy the product consistently in the future. Only if the quality of the product is so superior to others in the marketplace that it seems to outweigh price considerations will they purchase that product instead of the most inexpensive brand available.

Nonusers

Sampling is probably the best—and, in many cases, the only—tool that can convince nonusers of a particular product category to begin to use the product. Because samples are usually free, their use carries no financial risk. Once consumers try a product, there is a chance that they will like it and continue to purchase it in the future.

However, in most cases marketers should not expect a large growth in business from consumers who are not currently using any product in a particular category when a sampling promotion is run. Most nonusers have solid reasons for not buying a particular type of product—either they have no need for it or are simply not interested. Generally, only a product that is markedly superior to others on the market, or one that establishes a new category of its own, is likely to convince many nonusers of a category to become future buyers.

Sampling and Residual Market Value

Of all sales promotion techniques, sampling has the highest potential for creating residual market value. The purpose of sampling is to get consumers to try a product, making it more likely that they will purchase it in the future. The trade-off, however, is that sampling programs tend to be quite expensive and often do not provide profits over the short term. They therefore should be viewed as brand-building activities designed to increase profits into the future.

CHAPTER ELEVEN

Cause-Related Promotions

A growing form of sales promotion involves the contribution of funds to charitable institutions. Although monetary donations to not-for-profit organizations have often been categorized as public or community relations activities, many companies have recently attempted to use them to sell more product or create consumer goodwill by tying them to product sales. For example, a cereal manufacturer might donate 10 cents to a U.S. Olympic Team for every box of the product sold, or a retailer may donate a small percentage of sales from consumers who request it to a particular local charity.

Sales promotions that link charitable causes to product purchases have become increasingly popular in recent years, probably because they combine some of the best features of public relations and sales promotions. Promotions of this type generate positive feelings among consumers, but they tend to be even better at this than straight charitable contributions because they draw attention to the cause and allow consumers to feel good about themselves (and therefore about the sponsoring organization) without having to contribute money out of their own pockets.

In addition, in certain circumstances charitable programs can be quite successful in encouraging consumers to buy a particular brand. For example, in 1995 almost 70 percent of consumers reported having purchased brands because of a connection to a

Exhibit 11.1   A Cause-Related Promotion

Source: Courtesy of McNeil Consumer Products Company.

worthy cause, and 66 percent said they would switch brands in order to support a cause-related effort. As a result, 91 percent of retailers and 58 percent of packaged-goods manufacturers in 1995 reported having recently used cause-related programs to promote their products.

Uses of Cause-Related Promotions

Charitable promotions are becoming increasingly popular and can be particularly effective in certain circumstances. For example, they can be very successful at persuading consumers to choose one product over another when it appears that there is little differentiation in the category and when price discounting by all the players has become common. U.S. Sprint, for instance, has donated a percentage of its sales to the environment, in order to provide a point of differentiation in the competitive long-distance telephone-service business. Dominick's, a supermarket chain in Chicago, offers local charitable organizations a chance to hold promotions where a percentage of all sales to the group's supporters on a particular day is donated to the charitable group. This type of promotion may be successful not only at persuading consumers to

Exhibit 11.2 A Promotion Offering Funds to Local Causes

switch brands, but also to increase their usage (for instance, by making more phone calls or stocking up on groceries).

In categories where all products appear to be basically the same, charitable promotions can sometimes be even more effective than price discounting. When consumers get a small price reduction, they may not consider it to be very significant. But if the same amount is donated to a good cause, they may feel positive about their purchase and focus not just on the small donation from their own purchase but on the accumulated donations from the product sold. For instance, the promise that "McDonald's will donate 5 percent of all sales to the 'Make a Wish Foundation' for terminally ill youngsters, or a minimum of $500,000" may be significantly more attractive than "Ten cents off on all burgers!"

Another advantage of cause-related promotions is that they tend to be relatively easy to implement compared to other sales promotions. Most promotional programs, for example, involve significant administrative expenses. In addition, some programs (such as sweepstakes and contests) are subject to considerable legal restrictions while others (such as special packs and coupons) require retailer participation if they are to be successful. In contrast, cause-related promotions are a model of simplicity: after communicating to consumers through advertising, public relations,

Exhibit 11.3   A Charitable Promotion Appealing to a Brand's
Target Audience

Source: Courtesy of Weight Watchers.

or packaging that the donation will be made, all the manufacturer needs to do is add up the number of units of the product sold during the promotional period and send a check to the charity.

Cause-related promotions may be especially appropriate for some products or consumer targets. Young people, for instance, have often responded favorably to such promotions in recent years. In addition, if the target of the donation is of interest to the product's target audience, consumer response can be particularly good. For instance, Ben & Jerry's, a super-premium ice cream that appeals to young, upscale, environmentally conscious consumers, has donated money to preserve Brazilian rain forests. Nike, a sneaker brand popular in inner cities, has supported educational programs targeted at African Americans. Levi Strauss, whose jeans are popular in the gay community, has given money to AIDS research.

Other successful cause-related promotions attempt to reinforce the benefits of the brand through the careful selection of related charitable institutions. For example, The Body Shop, an organization that has made extensive use of cause-related promotions, reinforces the idea that its cosmetic products are made from natural ingredients by donating money to environmental organizations. Ajax, a manufacturer of cleaning products, has created programs that employ young people to clean up communities in inner cities. Purina has demonstrated its concern for all felines, large and small, by donating money to protect endangered species of "big cats."

Exhibit 11.4   A Cause-Related Promotion Tied to a Brand Benefit

Source: Courtesy of Colgate-Palmolive Company.

Exhibit 11.5   A Cause-Related Promotion Tied to
Coupon Usage

Source: Courtesy of SC Johnson Wax.

Developing Cause-Related Promotions

Usually, but not always, marketers tend to choose relatively non-controversial charitable organizations for their cause-related promotions. Many companies, for example, might shy away from donating money to Planned Parenthood, since a sizable group of consumers object to the abortion-related services that the organization provides. In some circumstances, however, a company with a specifically targeted consumer base may choose to support a controversial cause that is important to the people who buy its products. In that case, the organization may be applauded by its customers for its bravery and may receive additional long-term goodwill from them.

Whatever type of charitable cause is selected, it is usually helpful for companies to select one or more specific organizations and promote their names in all advertising of the cause-related promotion. Otherwise, some cynical consumers may doubt whether the organization will actually make the promised donations, and some of the goodwill and sales that otherwise would have been gained from the promotion may be lost.

Most of the time, companies use cause-related promotions to market items that are part of their regular line of products. In other situations, however, organizations may develop special products for a particular cause-related promotion. For instance, General Mills developed Team USA Cheerios prior to the 1996 Olympic Games and donated money to the U.S. team for each of the first million boxes sold. The creation of special products may draw particular attention to the fact that a specific cause is being supported, and therefore may create an especially large amount of consumer goodwill.

The amount of money donated to the charitable organization is usually tied to sales of the product (for instance, 10 cents per unit sold or 5 percent of all after-tax products), although sometimes it may be determined by other measures, such as the number of coupons redeemed. A minimum or maximum amount of money that will be donated to the charitable organization also may be specified.

Strategic Uses of Cause-Related Promotions

Cause-related promotions tend to be best at encouraging immediate sales when individuals have relatively little preference about which brand to purchase. Compared to other sales promotion tactics, they tend to be especially good at increasing long-term brand equity, since they help to establish a caring image for the organization and, in some situations, reinforce brand benefits.

Loyal Users

Cause-related promotions can be especially appropriate when companies want to target people who are already loyal to their products. These kinds of promotions can make people feel better about purchasing the products they already use, making them more resistant to overtures from competitors in the future. For example, an individual who usually purchases skin-care products from The Body Shop may feel guilty about switching to another brand that is not known for making donations to charitable organizations. In addition, well-chosen cause-related promotions can create an overall impression that companies are "good guys" and care about issues that are relevant to their consumers.

In addition, cause-related promotions may sometimes encourage loyal users to make additional purchases. This may be especially likely when extra product is desirable to consumers (that is, when category demand is elastic), as may be the case with items such as ice cream, fast foods, and cosmetics, all of which have used cause-related promotions successfully.

Competitive Loyals

People who regularly purchase a competitive product because they have a special affection for its benefits or image are generally not the best targets for cause-related promotions. This is likely to be the case because they may consider the donation made to the charitable organization to be insignificant compared to inducements that companies have offered them to switch in the past. However, consumers who purchase a particular brand out of habit may be persuaded to try another brand, at least on a one-time basis, especially if they are concerned about the cause being patronized and if they feel that switching will produce no long-run harm. For example, people who usually buy Ragu spaghetti sauce may decide to try Newman's Own if they learn that the latter brand donates its after-tax profits to charitable organizations. Similarly, a consumer who has previously been loyal to Clinique skin-care products may purchase a trial-sized item from The Body Shop because of that organization's charitable donations; if it proves to be satisfactory, more purchases may follow.

Switchers

Cause-related promotions can be excellent incentives for brand switchers, since they give people a good reason to purchase one specific product in the category. If the charitable organization being supported is an attractive one to the consumers being targeted, these kinds of promotions can be an especially useful means of appealing to switchers, since they may be implemented at a lower cost than many other kinds of sales promotions. In addition, since consumers may develop a favorable impression of companies that support worthy causes, they sometimes continue to purchase the brand even after the promotion is over.

Exhibit 11.6 A Charitable Promotion in a Competitive Category

Source: Courtesy of Kimberly-Clark Corporation and McDonald's Corporation.

Price Buyers

Cause-related promotions generally do little to attract price buyers to a product. This type of consumer tries to buy the least expensive product in a category, and other lower-priced alternatives to the brand using the cause-related promotion usually are readily available. Even if these cost-conscious consumers want to support a particular cause, they may decide that it is more rational to send the organization a check rather than funnel the money through a marketing organization.

Nonusers

Cause-related promotions usually do little to persuade nonusers of a particular product to purchase it. Even if consumers are especially concerned about a particular cause, they generally find it more gratifying to donate money directly to the organization than buy a product they don't want.

There may be some exceptions to this general statement, however. For instance, many people will buy cookies, candy, or other items from youngsters raising money for youth activities, even if they don't really need the products or intend to use them. However, this probably works because the purchasers want to help the children feel they have made a sale. The same principle therefore may not be applicable to products sold through regular consumer-products channels.

The Residual Value of Cause-Related Promotions

Cause-related promotions tend to have substantial residual value, since they can persuade consumers to think well of the organizations that offer them. This may be especially true when targeted consumers identify with the organization being supported. In addition, as noted, some cause-related promotions are successful at reinforcing the primary selling message of the brand, which also can increase brand value. Finally, in some cases, cause-related promotions may persuade consumers to try new products, and it is possible that these individuals will continue to use the product after the promotion has come to an end.

CHAPTER TWELVE

Price Discounts

Price discounts give consumers an immediate reduction on the amount they have to pay for the product at the point of purchase. Discounts given by the retailer are called "markdowns" (or simply "sale prices"), while discounts offered by the manufacturer of a product that is sold through a separate retailer are called "price-offs."

Retailers offer price reductions to consumers for a variety of reasons. The most common is to clear the firm's inventory of excess merchandise, so that new items may be warehoused and displayed. Retailers also use price reductions to attract consumers who might buy other products in their stores, and to create an overall low-price image for themselves.

Manufacturer price-offs flag products on the store shelf so that consumers will notice that they are receiving an immediate discount. For example, a flag, banner or burst on the package label may read "Save 50 cents" or "Price of product is 75 cents off." Although they can be useful in certain situations, price-offs have been used by manufacturers with decreasing frequency in recent years.

Retailer Price Discounts

Retailer price discounts may be used to accomplish a number of goals. Most importantly for many firms, they can help dispose of inventory remaining from previous seasons, allowing the retailer to move new merchandise into stores and warehouses. Price discounts for this purpose tend to be used most frequently by companies that make substantial changes in their selection of merchandise over time. For example, clothing stores often offer end-of-season sales, and car dealers give discounts on older vehicles when new models are released. Retailers who offer discounts in order to clear excess merchandise often attempt to keep prices high enough to cover what they originally paid for the product, but in some cases they will sell a product at a loss simply to dispose of it.

Another frequent use of price discounts is to encourage consumers to visit a particular retailer, in the hope that they will purchase other items while they are in the store. This type of strategy tends to be used primarily by retailers such as grocery, drug, and discount stores, where consumers tend to buy a large number of items while in the store. Retailers using price discounts to accomplish this goal may offer particular products as "loss leaders"—sold at a lower price than the retailer paid for it—in order to create a particularly attractive promotion that will bring more consumers into the store. Some retailers of higher-end products, such as appliances, also use heavily discounted prices on certain items to lure consumers into the store; once the customers are there, salespeople may point out the limitations of the sale item and attempt to sell them a higher-end model. However, this use of price discounting, commonly known as "bait and switch," is generally perceived as unethical and may alienate customers. In addition, if the discounted item is not readily available, the advertising may also be found to be illegal.

Retailers may also offer sale prices that are at least slightly above their own costs in order to price-discriminate between different kinds of consumers. For example, retailers of window coverings often offer prices that fluctuate dramatically over time due to periodic heavy discounting. This type of approach may make it possible for a particular retailer to target both price-sensitive and price-insensitive consumers, extracting maximum profits from both groups. Under this kind of pricing plan, many people who are relatively unconcerned about price may buy the product when it is not on sale, giving the company a higher profit margin. On the other hand, consumers who are determined to pay less buy when the product is on sale rather than purchasing from a competitive retailer. By contrast, a store offering a single, moderate price at all times may end up losing price-conscious consumers (who would be likely to choose a competitor offering rock-bottom prices during a sale) as well as making less money than it could have made selling to consumers who are less price-sensitive. While this pricing strategy may seem to be inherently exploitive of some consumers' lack of information about a particular product category, some retailers defend it by saying that individuals who are relatively price-insensitive save time in search costs and (because they make their purchases during times when stores are less busy) may also receive better service than people who buy when the product is on sale.

Retailers may sometimes offer products at a discount in order to counteract or preempt threats from competitors who are either entering a market or who are also running a special promotion. Such measures are usually legal, provided that the companies running them are not selling products below cost in an attempt to eliminate competition from the marketplace.

Finally, retailers may offer frequent promotions on products in order to create a low-price image for their brand or simply to increase sales during a specific period. While the idea that their merchandise is low-priced is exactly what some retailers want to avoid, stores that target price-conscious consumers may find it is beneficial to communicate the idea that good values exist in the store. The Limited, for example, has offered frequent discounts on much of its merchandise, including clothing that is still in season, communicating the idea that the stores offer good value.

Limitations of Retailer Price Discount

While discounting can help retailers to fulfill specific goals, many observers think too-frequent price promotions make consumers more price-sensitive and unwilling to buy any products in the category at full price in the future. For example, a number of clothing-store chains have observed that many shoppers believe that "everything will go on sale eventually," and tend to postpone purchases of items they would otherwise have bought at full price until they can get a discount. This may especially be true when consumers live near a number of outlets of a particular retail chain, such as Victoria's Secret or The Gap, since they believe that if an

Exhibit 12.1   A Retailer Discount Offer

Source: Courtesy of Walgreens.

item sells out at one store they may be able to find it at another. In addition, people who pay full price for an item can become annoyed if it soon goes on sale; in order to pacify these people, some stores even refund these customers the difference between the regular and the sale price if they bring in their sales receipts within a certain time. When this occurs, the promotion causes the retailer to lose profits retroactively on items that have already been sold.

A number of suggestions have been proposed for retailers who have found that too-frequent discounting in order to clear excess merchandise has eroded their core sales. An obvious solution is to make better buying decisions so that less merchandise is left over at the end of the selling period. However, most marketers find this is easier said than done. Another possibility is to dispose of the merchandise at another location, so that it will be seen only by consumers who actively seek it out and seem more divorced from the full-price merchandise. For example, Coach, a manufacturer of expensive handbags, sells its excess inventory at a few stores in outlet malls, while its regular stores rarely feature sale merchandise.

Another trick that has sometimes been proposed is for retailers to display fewer items at one time. For example, a woman who sees only one size 8 dress of a particular style hanging on the rack at Ann Taylor may be more likely to purchase it at full price than if she sees four such garments. (Such a strategy may work less well, however, once consumers realize that the stores have additional merchandise in the back room and ask the sales staff about the status of particular items.) Another strategy that might make consumers less price-sensitive is to state the discount in terms other than the percentage off the original price—for instance, "$10 Off" or simply "All Items $20" rather than "30% Off." Another possibility is to offer multiple units of the product at a low price, a technique that may encourage consumers to buy additional merchandise. For example, General Nutrition Centers often has "Buy One, Get One at Half-Price" deals on its vitamin products in the hope that consumers will see that they are getting a good deal and stock up. However, such programs run the risk of annoying consumers if only one unit of the desired product is in stock, unless some compensation that is acceptable to all consumers is made.

Everyday Low Pricing (EDLP)

Perhaps in reaction to the heavy price promoting that occurs in many categories, a variety of companies that sell products directly to consumers have experimented with everyday low-pricing (EDLP) formats. This type of pricing policy offers prices that are consistent over time. EDLP retailers tend to offer prices that are somewhat higher than their "hi-low" competitors' sales prices, but are considerably lower than those firms' standard prices. Everyday low-pricing strategies have been tried in industries ranging from grocery stores and airlines to car companies and appliance stores.

Everyday low-pricing strategies seem to have the potential of being attractive to consumers because they may minimize the amount of time people spend searching for a low price. In practice, however, this pricing policy tends to work better in some circumstances than in others. First, everyday low pricing may work best for firms that have lower built-in costs than their competitors, since they are able to offer regular prices that are relatively competitive with other companies' sale prices. For example, Wal-Mart, Best Buy, Home Depot, and Southwest Airlines are among the companies that have worked to reduce operational costs, and this is reflected in the everyday prices they offer consumers. On the other hand, Sears, which tried an everyday low-pricing strategy in the early 1990s, found that its high cost structure at that time did not allow it to offer competitive prices, and the effort was basically abandoned.

Another instance when everyday low prices may be effective is when a similar product is not readily available at other retailers. For example, General Motors' Saturn division required all its dealers to agree to no-discount pricing on its cars when it began doing business in the early 1990s. Although this "everyday low pricing" approach worked for Saturn, it was less successful for car companies that had been in business longer, since their dealers were not contractually obligated to refrain from dealing on price.

Finally, everyday low pricing may be effective when consumers are relatively unconcerned about prices and value their time more than any money they might save by shopping around for alternatives. For example, retailers such as Nordstrom that cater to upscale shoppers offer few sales, since their customers often are willing to pay a relatively high price in order to avoid the tedium of comparison shopping. On the other hand, during recessions or when money seems tight, many consumers may be willing to shop around more to get a good deal. It then may be less likely that everyday low-price strategies will attract much business.

Everyday low-pricing policies have had mixed success in the grocery industry. While a number of chains have attempted to decrease the use of price promotions, most have found it necessary to offer at least some items on special every week to attract the large contingent of people who scan store circulars and buy other items once they are in a particular store. In 1995, only about 14 percent of grocery stores offered EDLP formats, compared to 41 percent that offered promotional (hi-low) pricing and 45 percent that said they had attempted to cut back on the number and size of the discounts offered but still used a limited number of them on a regular basis.

Manufacturer Price-Offs

Price-offs given by manufacturers flag products on the store shelf so that consumers will realize they are getting an immediate dis-

Exhibit 12.2   Price-Off: On the Label

Source: Courtesy of Hunt-Wesson Foods, Inc.

count on the price. Like discounts offered by companies that sell directly to consumers, manufacturer price-offs give consumers a break on the price of a product automatically, without requiring them to do anything (such as use a coupon or send in a refund certificate) to "earn" it. However, manufacturers who wish to offer price-offs to consumers face specific complications, because these promotions require the cooperation and support of the retailers involved.

Uses of Price-Offs

The most obvious benefit of price-offs is that they provide a differentiating factor to consumers at the point of purchase. Consumers who are price-sensitive may notice the flagged package on the store shelf and decide to buy the promoted product rather than a competing brand because of the discount. Therefore price-offs may influence consumers more effectively than simply lowering the price of the product, because the flag on the product is likely to catch the attention of people who otherwise might not have bothered to compare the prices of all the products in the category.

In addition, price-offs are very flexible for the manufacturer, who can easily control the number of promoted products released into the marketplace. Since the marketer has control over the number of units that are distributed and the geographic area in which the offer will be made, price-offs can be helpful "fire-fighting" tools to counter competitive threats in certain marketplaces and at certain times. They also can be used to boost sales of a particular package size, flavor, or brand in a line. For example, if the large size of a product needs a boost, a price-off can be added only to that size to encourage purchases.

Another attractive feature of price-offs to some manufacturers is that, because the company has control over the number of products being distributed, the cost of the promotion can be predicted upfront. This differs from other consumer promotions such as coupons or rebates, where it may be difficult to predict the redemption rate.

However, price-offs also have a number of disadvantages, which explains why they are used less frequently than many other types of promotions. For example, consumers may not always believe that the marked price is "really" discounted, particularly if it is still more expensive than that of competitive products. In addition, laws require that the "regular" price referred to in the price-off must actually be the one charged for the product a certain percentage of the time, which can make price-offs difficult to administer. In addition, if price-offs are used too frequently, they may help to downgrade the image of the brand, so that some consumers begin to believe that it is not "worth" the undiscounted price. This may eventually mean that the product will sell only when it is on discount, thereby cutting into long-term profits.

Another major issue is that, unlike coupons, price-offs are automatically given to all consumers who buy a product, whether or not they would have ordinarily purchased it. This factor may mean that price-offs occasionally will be superior to coupons in prompting sales, because they may appeal to consumers who don't use coupons. However, unlike coupons, price-offs have no ability to price-tier—that is, to offer varying prices to different consumers based on their price-sensitivity. Price-offs therefore are often reserved for categories where most consumers are price-sensitive, such as paper towels or dishwashing soap. They also often are restricted to relatively low dollar amounts.

Even more importantly, price-offs have been relatively unpopular with the trade, with less than 50 percent of all food and drug retailers accepting them in their stores. For one thing, retailers must handle products with price-off banners separately from regular-priced merchandise (some of which may already be in stock) in the warehouse and on the store shelf, and must make sure that the amount charged for the product actually reflects the price reduction. In addition, unlike trade discounts (which are often passed on to the consumers as advertised "specials"), price-offs do nothing to generate store traffic for retailers.

In addition, some retailers don't like price-off promotions from manufacturers because they can reduce profits on a particular product. For example, most retailers calculate their profits based on what they pay for the product. Thus, if they buy a product for 50 cents and take a 20 percent margin, the retail price of the product to the consumer, or the shelf price, would be 60 cents. When a manufacturer reduces the price of the product by a set amount through a price-off, however, the retailer's margin is also reduced, unless an adjustment is made.

Price-offs also provide special handling problems for the manufacturer. Since price-off packs must be a separate manufacturing run (or must include a special sticker announcing the price reduction), production costs of materials and processing often increase. Also, because the promotion must be offered to all competitive retailers within a market area but may not be accepted by all of them, adequate supplies of both regular-priced and special merchandise must be readily available.

Because of these issues, the use of price-offs by manufacturers has been relatively limited. Price-off promotions are often used to overcome situations where the competition has introduced new or reformulated products or has made changes in pricing, packaging, trade or consumer sales promotions, advertising, or other promotional activities.

A device similar to price-offs is the use of a prominently featured "Manufacturer's Suggested Retail Price" on the box or package. This type of promotion may help to call attention to the fact that one product is priced lower than others in the category, and (unlike price-off flags) it can be used on a consistent basis rather than only a certain percentage of the time. However, since retailers are unlikely to accept a product marked with a suggested price lower than the one they intend to charge, the suggested price is usually on the high side, meaning that it is advantageous only when the price of the product is substantially lower than that of its competitors. The frequent use of such a tool may also, for good or bad, forever identify the product as a brand that appeals to consumers only on the basis of price.

Developing Price-Offs

Planning price-offs requires a great deal of coordination and cooperation throughout the entire manufacturing organization. Since the development of the price-off pack is essentially a manufacturing process (that is, special labels must be affixed or special containers used in the production run), the production department, the shipping and storage people, the sales force, the wholesaler, and the retailer must all be coordinated so that the promotion is carried out smoothly. A price-off is usually not something that can be developed overnight.

The method of display of the price-off offer on the package is critical to its success. While there is always concern with the attractiveness of the label or feature area, the clarity of the offer and its visibility on the shelf outweigh most aesthetic considerations. If the customer can't see the price-off, it simply won't work. A bold burst (a jagged-edge price spot) or flag (a box printed over the regular label) is best, with the amount clearly stated. The offer should not be hidden.

Generally, a direct price-off will produce the most sales action. The more complicated the price-off, the lower the interest in the promotion by the consumer.

Costs

Two cost factors should be considered when evaluating a price-off promotion. The first is the cost of the price reduction. This is a fairly straightforward calculation. Simply multiply the number of units on which the price-off is to be used by the amount of the reduction. For example, if the price is to be reduced 10 cents per unit on 100,000 units, the total costs of the reduction would be $10,000. An additional cost that is not quite so easy to calculate is that of the special labels and cartons. Since art work, plates, and special printing are involved, this cost will vary for almost every offer, depending on what is to be done. The production people are the ones most qualified to determine these costs.

Pricing

Price-offs must usually be a minimum of 15 to 20 percent off the regular price of the product in order to have much effect on sales. In general, brands with smaller market shares must offer larger reductions than brand leaders in order to achieve similar sales increases. As might be expected, larger reductions in price tend to attract more new triers at the retail level, while lower reductions tend to attract people who might have purchased the product even without the discount.

Estimating Supplies

While the supply of price-off units may be estimated on several different bases, it is typically figured as a certain number of weeks of estimated product movement. In other words, the number of price-off units to be offered is determined on the basis of previous or estimated week's sales. Let's assume that sales of Product Alpha have been 100 per week. The manufacturer estimates that sales will increase by 20 percent with the promotion. Thus if the promotion is planned to run 5 weeks, 600 units will be produced (100 units per week plus a 20 percent increase, or 120 units per week × 5 weeks). Usually a 4- to 8-week supply of the price-off merchandise is planned for the average promotion. If the promotion is not being offered in all areas, the promotion amount can be determined by using previous sales or shipments to the specific areas involved.

Federal Trade Commission Regulations

The Federal Trade Commission (FTC) regulations covering a price-off sales promotion program are quite specific. Generally, the FTC requires that:

1. Price-offs may be utilized only by brands with an established retail price.

2. No more than 50 percent of the total volume of a brand may be generated through price-offs in any 12-month period.

3. Only three price-off promotions per year are allowed on any one brand size. A 30-day period must also be allowed between each of the price-off offers on the brand.

4. A price-off must be accompanied by display material that gives the following information clearly:

Brand name	Brand X
Regular price	78¢
Cash savings	12¢
New price	66¢

Exhibit 12.3   Price-Off: On Flexible Packaging

Source: William A. Robinson, "Five More 'Best Promotions' Share the Facts and Shed Light on Marketing Success," *Advertising Age*, April 3, 1978, p. 52.

A retailer who uses this technique must indicate the regular price, the price reduction, and the new price.[1]

For other legal factors that may affect price-offs for the brand or category, legal counsel should be consulted. Also, the marketer

---

[1]Sales Promotion Committee, American Association of Advertising Agencies, *Sales Promotion Techniques: A Basic Guidebook* (New York: American Association of Advertising Agencies, 1978), 31-32.

must ascertain that all price-offs are in compliance with current regulations.

Designing Graphics

When designing a "burst" or a "flag," it is more important to get the price reduction across so shoppers can see it than to have the price look aesthetically pleasing. The only real requirement is that the price reduction not be so large that the general identification of the label is impaired.

Strategic Uses of Price Discounts

Price reductions have the advantage of being simpler for consumers to use than most other sales promotion tactics, since all individuals need to do to get the discount is to make a purchase. This form of promotion therefore may be attractive to consumers who are unwilling to invest much effort in obtaining price discounts, especially if those individuals already have an interest in the product being promoted.

Loyal Users

Current users of a brand tend to be particularly likely to respond to discounts on products offered at the point of purchase, since they may be more aware than most people that the price being offered is a good one. In many situations the attractiveness of discounts to current users of a brand may be a problem, since the discounted product that is moved may be cannibalizing sales that otherwise would be made at full price. However, depending on the product category and the disposition of the current users of the product, discounts may also encourage loyal users to increase their consumption of the product—for example, by getting them to eat more Oreos, purchase additional clothing, or trade in their car a year earlier. Because price discounts that appeal to current users can have positive or negative effects on the profitability of an organization's marketing efforts, it is important to attempt to predict how those individuals are likely to behave when discounts are available before implementing this type of promotional program.

Competitive Loyals

Discounts are often used by companies in order to get competitors' customers to make a purchase; in some cases, the trial gained from these people may lead to further purchases in the future. However, such discounts usually must be quite large in order to prompt these consumers to switch brands, and may result in an overall loss in profitability if increased sales are not enough to compensate for the loss on products that would have otherwise been sold at the regular price.

Switchers

People who use a variety of products in a category tend to be excellent targets for price discounts. Consumers who switch depending on which product seems to be the best value at the time are likely to notice and be motivated by a price discount, even if it is not particularly large. Consumers who switch because they enjoy using a variety of brands may view a price discount—particularly if it is displayed in a way that makes it particularly noticeable—as a tie-breaker that causes them to buy one product rather than another. Discounts designed to appeal to switchers should be developed to generate profits over the short run, however, since it is unlikely that they will make these people more likely to buy the product in the future.

Price Buyers

Depending on the size of the discount being offered, price reductions may be very successful in prompting price buyers to purchase a particular product. After the discount period is over, however, these people will generally go back to the brand that is the least expensive at the time of purchase. Therefore, it is important to ensure that discounts targeted to price buyers provide profitability over the short term or accomplish some other specific goal, such as helping to dispose of excess inventory.

Nonusers

Consumers who use no products in a particular category are generally unlikely to be attracted by discounts. In most cases, the consumers won't even be looking in the section of the stores where the product is sold, so they may not even notice the promotion, much less be influenced to buy the product. Only if the discount is particularly large and the lack of previous purchases was due solely to price considerations may discounts influence these individuals to buy.

Price Discounts and Residual Value

Of all sales promotion tactics, price discounts probably do the least for the value of a brand over the long term. Discounts tend to attract relatively little consumer trial of a product, meaning that few new sales are likely to be made after the brand goes back to its regular price. Also, excessive discounting of a product may suggest to consumers that the brand is not worth the full price, and they therefore may be unwilling to pay the full price for it in the future. In most cases, discounts should be evaluated in terms of short-term profitability only, unless the company has a specific reason that goes beyond increasing profitability (such as inventory reduction) for using them.

CHAPTER THIRTEEN

Trade Deals

Trade deals offer some sort of incentive, usually a lower price, to encourage the retailer to do something extra to promote a specific brand. Generally, trade allowances are designed to gain or maintain retail distribution, or to obtain retail price promotions, retail advertising, or retail displays.

Trade deals have become increasingly popular in recent years, and accounted for 51 percent of all packaged-goods marketing expenditures in 1995. This is largely due to the increasing power of retailers compared to that of manufacturers, a condition caused by declining consumer brand loyalty, product parity, surplus product, and increasing competition among manufacturers for consumer dollars. In order to attract consumer attention at the store level and to maintain the support of retailers, it has become increasingly important for manufacturers to offer various forms of incentives to retailers.

Here are some examples of trade allowances commonly offered by manufacturers:

- *Packaged goods*. Manufacturers offer price reductions to persuade retailers to stock up and pass savings along to consumers through lower shelf prices. Off-shelf display, advertising, or price reductions may sometimes be required as proof of performance.

- *Cosmetics.* Manufacturers pay for their own demonstrators and sales clerks, and for counter space in department stores. They also may pay "spiffs" as bonuses to retailers' own clerks for selling particular products in a line on a regular basis or during certain time periods.

- *Auto aftermarket.* Manufacturers offer discounts to whole-salers, who may or may not pass them on to retailers.

- *Housewares appliances.* Retailers deduct a "promotional allowance" from the invoice, and manufacturers accept certification that the funds were spent for promotions.

Trade Deals—the Manufacturer's View

Manufacturers may offer trade deals to retailers or wholesalers for two reasons. They may hope to gain short-term volume increases that improve their profits over what ordinarily would have been achieved. They may also hope that the use of trade promotions will increase the viability of the brand over the long term.

Usually, trade promotions are used to increase the volume being sold. When a trade discount is offered, the retailer in effect gets a "sale" price and is thus likely to want to buy more of the product. In some cases retailers may stockpile the brand in their warehouses and use it up gradually, thereby eliminating the need to buy as much product later at the regular price. Often, however, retailers may increase their sales volume of the product and move it out of their warehouses immediately by passing some of the discount on to their customers in the form of a "special," causing consumers to buy more of the brand. In addition, retailers may call attention to the lower price by advertising it (for example, in a television or newspaper ad or in a store circular), by setting up a special display for the product in the store, or by calling attention to it at its regular location on the store shelf with a small sign known as a "shelf talker."

Occasionally, manufacturers may benefit from getting retailers to "forward buy" and stockpile merchandise due to a trade discount. For example, a company that has a specific financial or volume goal to meet during a particular quarter or year may choose to load up the trade, even if it means that the organization will sacrifice sales later on. In general, however, for the promotion to be considered a success, it is necessary for at least part of the discount to be passed on to the consumer, thereby increasing retail sales.

For a trade promotion to be judged profitable in the long run, it is necessary that the manufacturer's increase in sales offset the manufacturer's decrease in margin. In addition, it is important to look not only at how much product would ordinarily have been sold during the promotional period, but also at the amount of sales after (and sometimes before) the promotional period that were "cannibalized" by retailers' or consumers' stockpiling the product for use in later periods (or, sometimes, by their allowing inventory to shrink in anticipation of replacing it with product on deal).

For instance, assume that Super Market, a grocery store, would ordinarily purchase 10 units of Brand X each month during January, February, and March at a profit of $10 per unit to the manufacturer; total profits would therefore be $300. Now, assume that Brand X held a trade promotion during February, reducing the manufacturer's margin to $5 per unit. If Super Market took the opportunity to stockpile the brand while it was on deal, its purchases might be 10 units in January, 20 units in February, and 0 units in March. This would result in a net profit of $200 for Brand X—or $100 less than the company would have earned if no trade deal had been offered.

Now assume that instead of stockpiling the product, Super Market chooses to run an advertised special on it, passing on some of the manufacturer's discount to consumers. If that were to occur, purchases by Super Market might be 10 units in January, 50 units in February, and 10 units in March—for a total of $450 in profits for Brand X. Since this is much higher than the $300 that would have been earned with no promotion, this particular activity would be judged profitable and therefore successful for the manufacturer. The retailer, however, might or might not make a profit on the promotion, depending on the price that was offered to the consumer. Obviously, then, it is important to the manufacturer for the retailer to pass on part of its trade discount to consumers if such a promotion is to be judged profitable for the manufacturer.

Some experts believe that, in addition to short-term profits, trade promotions are capable of providing long-term benefits to manufacturers. For instance, trade promotions can sometimes provide an incentive for retailers to begin or continue to stock a particular brand. In addition, displays or trade advertising may generate attention for a brand, keeping it in the consumer's "evoked set." Trade promotions may also be helpful at warding off competitive threats by preventing another brand from getting retailer support in the immediate future or by loading retailers and consumers with products.

On the other hand, trade promotions can be negative to the perceived value and perhaps the image of brands, especially if they are offered too often.

Trade Deals—the Retailer's View

To understand how to work with retailers on trade promotions, it is important for manufacturers to know what motivates retailers, especially since their behavior in maximizing profit may not always produce the best possible results for the manufacturer.

No matter what type of store is being operated, retailer profits are affected by three major factors: (1) store traffic, or the number of people who come into the store; (2) volume, or how much each shopper, on average, buys from the store; and (3) profit margin, or how much money, on average, the retailer makes on what is sold.

Unlike manufacturers, retailers do not really care which brands consumers purchase while in the store, as long as those products have the same margin. Instead, they are interested in how much money they are making on each customer's "basket" of products and in the total number of customers who visit the store.

Therefore, before retailers will decide to promote a brand (that is, reduce its price, give it display space, and/or advertise it), they are likely to look at the following issues:

1. *Will promoting this item bring business into my store?* Some products, such as coffee or tuna fish, are used by a wide variety of consumers and have relatively high purchase prices. Running promotions on these products may cause many consumers to come to the store specifically to take advantage of the savings that are offered on these products. The retailer's hope is that, once in the store, these people will also purchase other, regular-priced products, thereby boosting total sales and profits for the retailer.

2. *What will running this promotion do to the total sales of the category?* Some products, such as toilet paper, have a finite total demand. Consumers may well take advantage of the low price on a particular brand, but this will usually be at the expense either of sales of other brands in the category (for instance, if the price of

Charmin is discounted, the sales of Northern may drop to almost nothing) or of future sales (if consumers stock up, they may not need to buy any more toilet paper for the next month). Deals on other types of products (such as ice cream) may, on the other hand, cause some consumers who wouldn't have ordinarily purchased any product to do so, creating extra total sales for the retailer. In general, retailers are more likely to run promotions that encourage consumers to make additional purchases, rather than to stock up or to switch from one brand to another. (Nevertheless, some retailers do frequently run specials on items like toilet paper, to lure customers into the store, to develop a "low price" image for the store, or to preempt or counter activity from competitive retailers.)

3. *How difficult or expensive would it be for me to store extra product?* A retailer who gets a deal on a bulky product such as paper towels, or on a perishable one such as milk, is likely to find it inefficient or impossible to warehouse the extra product. In that case, the retailer will be more likely to promote it, in order to get it off his hands. In other cases where product can be stored inexpensively, stockpiling may be common.

4. *If I promote this item, how much of a discount should I offer?* When determining how much to discount the price of a brand, retailers take into consideration their current margin on the brand, the discount being given to them by the manufacturer, and the potential for increased brand and category sales. Retailers will sometimes lower the price of a product by more than the discount they are getting from the manufacturer, but they will more commonly pass on only part of the manufacturer discount.

In the retailer's decision to promote or not promote a particular product, the answers to these price, volume, and margin questions are generally much more important than any persuasive actions on the part of the manufacturer. By keeping these issues in mind, manufacturers are more likely to be able to create trade promotions that are likely to have an impact on total sales over time.

Manufacturers may sometimes offer trade deals to retailers simply to obtain or maintain distribution. Usually, however, they hope that the trade deal will increase sales to the consumer by getting the retailer to offer a price discount on the product, to advertise it in the media or in store circulars, or to put it on display.

Price discounts generally have a large effect on the sales of brands to consumers, especially if they are advertised or featured in some way. Retailers can offer price discounts by reducing the amount charged for the brand (either to all consumers or to those enrolled in the store's frequent-shopper club), by offering an in-store coupon, or by giving extra product (for instance, "two for the price of one").

Trade advertising is generally paired with price discounts, increasing the number of people who become aware of the special and increasing the likelihood that they will visit the store to take advantage of it. Retailers may mention the special on the brand in television or radio commercials, in print advertising, or in store circulars. In some cases print advertising may include a trade coupon, which must be presented to the retailer in order to receive the discount.

Displays in the retail store draw attention to particular brands. Although displays can be successful at moving additional product at the regular price by attracting the attention of hurried shoppers, they are often paired with discounts to encourage maximum sales increases. Displays for brands may be located at the front of the store, at the end of an aisle, or in an aisle; in addition, "shelf talkers" may call attention to the brand at its regular spot on the shelf. Displays are often awarded to large, bulky products, since it might be difficult to store enough on the shelf to satisfy consumer demand for the product at a reduced price.

Types of Trade Discounts

Discounts may be offered to retailers in a number of ways. Some of these discounts force retailers to meet certain requirements, such as providing proof of advertising or displays; others have no such requirements.

In this section, to simplify the discussion, it is assumed that the manufacturer sells directly to the retailer with no wholesaler or distributor involved. However, in many cases trade promotions are developed by the manufacturer and offered to the wholesaler, who may choose to improve the offers or decide not to pass any of the discount on to the consumer. For the sake of clarity, we simplify the steps here rather than attempting to explain this complex world of multiple discounts. The basic concepts of each type of trade promotion then can be adjusted to fit individual buying categories and various methods of product distribution.

Buying Allowance

The buying allowance is simply a discount on the purchase of a brand at a certain time. For example, the manufacturer might offer the retailer a buying allowance of $1 per case for all cases purchased during the month of November. However, a buying allowance is often tied to the purchase of a certain number of units. For example, the manufacturer's buying allowance of $1 per case might be allowed on all purchases if 10 or more cases are purchased at one time. Or it might apply to all cases the retailer purchases in excess of the average purchased during the same period the previous year. In most instances the allowance is either deducted from the invoice or given as credit.

Usually, the purpose of a buying allowance is simply to gain or retain distribution or attempt to present a lower shelf price to the consumer. Often it is used to ward off competition or to load retailers prior to an anticipated competitive trade deal. While this kind of offer can be instituted quickly and easily and requires no special handling by the manufacturer, it does not require the retailer to promote the offer in any way or to pass the savings along to the consumer. Thus, while the objective of the manufacturer might be to obtain retail price features at the store level, the retailer may absorb the discount or allowance and take it as extra margin on the product. Therefore, although the buying allowance tends to be the most popular form of trade allowance, it often results in the least action at the consumer level.

Off-Invoice Allowance

While the buying allowance usually applies to some form of quantity discount, the off-invoice allowance normally refers to a price reduction for a certain period of time. For example, again assume that the manufacturer offers a $1 per case allowance. In this instance, however, the discount is allowed on all purchases made between March 1 and April 15. It makes no difference how many cases the retailer purchases, but the purchases must be made between those dates to earn the discount. In addition, the allowance is deducted directly from the invoice for the products. For example, if the product regularly sold for $10 per case and the retailer purchased 100 cases, the cost would be $1,000. With an off-invoice allowance, however, the manufacturer would submit an invoice for $1,000 less the $100 ($1 per case on 100 cases), making a net invoice to the retailer of $900.

Exhibit 13.1   Trade Allowance: Free Goods

Source: Courtesy of Duro-Lite Lamps, Inc.

This sort of promotion can be attractive because it is simple to use for both the retailer and the manufacturer. The basic difficulty for manufacturers is that the retailer may stockpile the product at the reduced price to sell later at a greater margin.

Free Goods

In a free-goods offer, the manufacturer offers an additional "free" amount of the product with the purchase of a minimum quantity. A typical offer might be to give one case free with the purchase of 12—a "baker's dozen." Normally, the free-goods offer is for a limited time and may or may not be for a one-time purchase. For example, the offer might be for the period May 1 through July 15, or it might be limited to the next order the retailer places within a certain time.

Manufacturers particularly like the free-goods offer because the only cost is the product being offered. This is actually the lowest net cost discount that the manufacturer can give. Here's why: Assume the cost to manufacture the product is $5 per case, and the normal wholesale price to the retailer is $10 per case. If the offer of one free case with the purchase of 10 were made, the discount cost per case on the product sold would be only 50 cents (10 cases are sold; one free case at a cost of $5 is given in the deal; $5 ÷ 10 cases = 50 cents per case). On the other hand, a buying allowance or off-invoice allowance would normally amount to more—for example, the $1 per case allowance mentioned above. While the free-goods offer in our example sounds much more impressive than the offer of 50 cents off per case, it actually amounts to the same net income to the manufacturer.

Some manufacturers also prefer the free-goods allowance because it may encourage the retailer to purchase more during a specific period of time. As a result of a free-goods allowance, retailers can often be encouraged to pass part of the savings along to the consumer.

A free-goods allowance can be an excellent trade promotion for many types of products. It doesn't tend to work well, however, on slow-moving items, since most retailers won't stock up on or promote a product that will only sell a few units per store each week.

Dating

Though technically not a form of trade allowance, dating is included here because it involves a form of discount or method of dealer allowance. *Dating* means that the retailer can obtain the product at one point in time and be billed for it in installments, although in some cases purchases may be made at a reduced price and shipped at a later date. For example, assume that a retailer purchases $750 worth of merchandise from a manufacturer on June 1. With dating, the retailer might pay $250 on August 1, another $250 on September 1, and the final $250 on October 1. In effect, the manufacturer is financing the purchase, but at no interest.

Dating is typically done on fairly high-priced, slow-moving items, such as tires, batteries, and some larger appliances; it can be a particularly good way to move seasonal products. Manufacturers may find the idea of dating attractive because it is a fairly inexpensive way of merchandising these kinds of products to the trade. In addition, it often helps marketers to save warehousing costs because product is moved out of their plants and into retailers' warehouses. On the other hand, some manufacturers, particularly those who sell high-volume products, avoid dating programs because they are essentially financing retailers to sell their products.

Cash Rebate

With the cash rebate, the manufacturer agrees to give the retailer a cash discount of some sort, provided that the retailer completes a mutually agreed-upon task. This may be simply to stock the product, to increase its shelf space, or to purchase and display a full product line. When proof of the performance of the task is provided, the manufacturer sends the retailer a check for the amount of the discount. In some cases, too, retailers may receive an annual rebate consisting of a fixed percentage of all purchases made throughout the year or of all purchases over a specific amount. For instance, in January, retailers may receive a 2 percent discount on all purchases over $100,000 made throughout the previous year.

The major advantage of cash rebates for manufacturers is that retailers must perform prior to payment. This enables the manufacturer to make sure the terms are fulfilled. However, a problem may occur if the retailer wants the money in advance, before performance is completed. This may present a difficult situation for the manufacturer, particularly if the retailer is a large account. In addition, ensuring that retailers have indeed performed may be cumbersome, particularly for manufacturers who sell through a large number of retailers.

Advertising or Display Allowance

Similar to the cash rebate is the advertising or display allowance. Again, the retailer must perform some function or service to earn the discount. The difference here is that normally the discount earned is in the form of a credit memo rather than cash. Additionally, the task to be performed by the retailer usually has to do with some sort of consumer offer, such as a display, a reduced-price special advertised in the newspaper, a price-off shelf feature, or the like. Usually, the advertising allowance requires the placement of space or time media to promote the product. The display requirement, on the other hand, normally involves in-store presentation of the product.

The advertising or display allowance is commonly written into a contract between the manufacturer and the retailer. As part of a contract, the advertising allowance is much easier to enforce, since the allowance need not be paid until after proof of performance is submitted. The proof usually consists of tear sheets of newspaper ads, copies of shelf signs, pictures of displays built, or other verification that the contract was completed.

For example, the manufacturer might give a $1.50 per case advertising allowance on a purchase if the retailer agrees to reduce the price of the product to the consumer and promote that price reduction in the outlet's regular newspaper advertisement. Usually, there are stipulations on how the advertisement must appear; that is, it must be a certain size, must appear within the main section of the newspaper ad, must be a price reduction below normal retail, and so on. The manufacturer cannot specify the amount of the reduction since this would amount to price fixing.

Other types of advertising or display allowances include a case or unit reduction for a feature with a shelf sign or a shelf-price reduction. Displays are usually rewarded on the basis of a flat amount per display or on a sliding scale based on the size of the display. There are literally hundreds of variations on the advertising and display allowance approach, and some are used more widely in certain product categories than in others.

The usual reason for an advertising or display allowance is to encourage some sort of retail activity in the store. It is also widely used to gain or hold retailers in the distribution system or to counter competitive activity.

Advertising or display allowances are generally easy for manufacturers to set up. Since they are established by contract, most retailers perform as expected. However, some retailers may try to take advantage of the contract and do only the minimum required. They may, for example, build only a few displays, or offer the smallest possible discount to the consumer. There is little the manufacturer can do about this if the retailer has complied with the actual terms of the contract; therefore, the language of the contract should be written carefully to avoid such loopholes or misunderstandings.

Scan Downs/Scan Backs

Scan downs and scan backs have become quite popular in recent years as most major supermarkets have adopted scanner technology. With this type of promotion, retailers receive a manufacturer's discount only on items sold during a particular time period. Information about the number of units sold is obtained from the retailers' scanner records. The advantage of this type of promotion for manufacturers is that promotional discounts are paid only on items sold, not on items stockpiled in the company's warehouse. Therefore, this type of promotion gives the retailer an incentive to pass along some or all of the discount to consumers, in order to maximize sales during the time period when the promotion is being offered.

Unlike the count-and-recount allowances used before scanner technology was available, scan downs/scan backs are relatively easy to administer. With count-and-recount allowances, manufacturers had to send representatives to company warehouses before and after promotions were administered to count the number of cases of goods in stock. Obviously, this type of documentation was expensive and tedious to obtain. Scanner data, on the other hand, make it relatively simple for manufacturers to determine the number of units that have moved through a store into consumers' hands over a set period of time, and to give discounts only on those items that are sold rather than on items stockpiled in the retailer's warehouse. The only potential problem with this kind of promotion is that retailers may not want to share this information with manufacturers, and that manufacturers may be wary of accepting the veracity of the numbers presented to them by retailers if trust between the two parties is not very strong.

Spiffs and Mystery Shopper Programs

Spiffs and mystery shopper programs attempt to influence the behavior of salespeople in categories where consumers making purchasing decisions rely on recommendations. In spiff programs, manufacturers pay members of the retailers' sales forces what amounts to a commission on every unit sold during a particular time period. "Mystery shoppers" visit stores anonymously and give gifts or cash to salespeople who recommend the "right" brand to them. (See Chapter 8 for more information on spiffs and mystery shopper programs.)

Slotting Allowances and Failure Fees

Although slotting allowances generally are used only for new rather than existing products, they have become an increasingly important element in retailer decisions about whether or not to stock new products.

In order to begin selling a new stockkeeping unit (that is, a new product or a new product size), retailers incur significant administrative expenses. For example, they must make room for the product in the warehouse (reserving a "slot" for it), must build it into their inventory systems, must reconfigure shelves in each of their stores to include the new item, and must reprogram their wholesale and retail computers. Since U.S. manufacturers introduce nearly 10,000 new products each year (including various sizes and varieties of new and existing products), these expenses can be significant.

The expenses and effort involved in incorporating new products or stockkeeping units (SKUs) into their stores can be particularly annoying to retailers because even successful new brands do not often cause consumers to buy more total product from a category. Instead, consumers shift their existing purchasing dollars to the new product. For instance, if a new brand of cookies is introduced, consumers may purchase the new brand rather than their old brand. Therefore, retailers have developed slotting allowances in an attempt to pass some of the administrative costs of stocking new brands back to the manufacturer.

Slotting allowances consist of one-time fees that retailers charge for the introduction of a new product, or a new size or flavor, into a store. Slotting allowances typically run $15–$25 per store; considering that there are approximately 30,000 major grocery stores in the United States, the amount of money manufacturers must pay in slotting allowances to introduce a new product nationwide can be considerable. Retailers defend these fees, however, by pointing out that in addition to covering their administrative costs, slotting allowances encourage manufacturers to introduce only those new products they are confident will succeed and are willing to promote.

An alternative to slotting allowances are the so-called "failure fees" paid by manufacturers if their recently introduced products must be removed from store shelves because of poor sales. Failure fees, which tend to be higher than slotting allowances, give manufacturers an extra incentive to introduce only products with high potential and to support their success.

Although slotting allowances generally must be paid by manufacturers of most new brands, they are sometimes waived by retailers who want to stock a particular item. These exceptions may include a size needed to round out a store's variety of products, a specialty item not manufactured by other companies, or a product that is certain to have high consumer demand.

Exhibit 13.2   Trade Coupons: In-Ad

Source: Courtesy of Walgreens Drug Stores.

Trade Coupons

Trade coupons are distributed by retailers and are good only on specific brands at the store offering the coupons. Trade coupons are usually valid for only a week or two, in order to get people into the store during a specific period of time.

Frequently, manufacturers will agree to reimburse the retailer a certain amount per coupon redeemed. Manufacturers may reimburse the retailer for the full face value of the coupon or for a percentage of it, depending on the agreement reached between the two parties. In addition, in order to be able to predict expenses more carefully and to control the number of retailer misredemptions, some manufacturers may fix limits on the number of coupons that will be reimbursed or on the total payment.

From the manufacturer's point of view, the primary advantage of trade coupons is the assurance that a proposed price reduction will be passed on to the consumer, and that it will be necessary to pay only for actual sales from price-sensitive consumers over a limited period of time. Retailers may see trade coupons as a way to maintain a low-price image, to generate store traffic, or to differentiate themselves from competition.

Trade coupons may be distributed by the retailer in a number of different ways. They may appear in ads, in coupon flyers, or in the store at the door or near the product.

Trade coupons may be especially effective in competitive situations. For example, a trade coupon featured by a major retailer may preclude the use of a competitive feature offered at the same time by other retailers in the market. Trade coupons may also work well at opening new territories or introducing new products, since customers may transfer acceptance from the retailer to the brand. In addition, trade coupons (unlike other trade promotions) are a guaranteed way to get a price reduction or other offer to the consumer.

Many retailers, however, have moved away from requiring that consumers present actual coupons; instead, they just give the discount to everyone purchasing the product. Although eliminating the need for the presentation of coupons can be convenient for retailers and consumers, it can make it more difficult for manufacturers to keep track of how many units were purchased. Scanner data may be helpful as a replacement.

Limitations of Trade Deals

Certain legal and practical considerations place constraints on the ways in which manufacturers can use trade promotions. For instance, it is illegal for manufacturers to require retailers to pass on any part of trade allowances to consumers. In addition, manufacturers must offer the same—or a proportionately equal—discount to all competing retailers within a defined geographic area, so discounts cannot be used to reinforce sales at some retailers but not others in a particular geographic area. (Volume discounts that allow larger retail chains to obtain bigger discounts than smaller retailers are permissible, however.) Diverters (agents who buy product at a discount in one area of the country, then resell it in other regions where it is not being promoted) also may make it impractical for manufacturers of most products to offer trade deals that vary substantially on a geographic basis.

Also, even though it is legal for manufacturers to require retailers to run advertising or display products in order to receive a trade deal, it may be difficult to monitor whether particular retailers actually conduct these activities. And even if the manufacturer determines that a particular retailer did not comply with a specific

Exhibit 13.3 Blattberg Trade Promotion Grid

	Retailer Holding Cost	
Consumer Price Elasticity	**High** **Great to Promote** • increased sales • little stockpiling (soft drinks, paper towels)	**High** **Huge Sales Spikes** • increased consumer sales • high retailer stockpiling (canned tuna, coffee)
	Low **Few Additional Sales** from Consumer or Retailers (dry dog food, bottled water)	**Low** **Awful to Promote** • few extra consumer sales • high retailer stockpiling (laxatives, spices)

Source: Developed by Robert C. Blattberg, Northwestern University.

requirement for a promotional allowance it may be hard to recoup that money without jeopardizing future trade relations.

Maximizing the Effectiveness of Trade Deals

Provided that they are passed on to consumers, trade deals can be very effective at drawing attention to a brand and creating a sharp spike in sales during a specific time period. However, trade deals tend to be most beneficial for manufacturers when they are run for relatively short time periods and at fairly infrequent intervals. If deals on a particular brand become too prevalent, both retailers and consumers may begin to see the discounted price as the regular price and therefore may become less responsive to future promotions and less willing to buy the brand when it is not on deal.

One positive feature of trade deals is that they can be implemented quickly; all that is necessary is to work out an agreement with retailers. They therefore can be effective in "fire-fighting" situations, such as when competitors have become more aggressive (by, for instance, increasing advertising or introducing a new brand) in a particular market.

Trade promotions tend to work best when brands being promoted have high holding or storage costs for the retailer, and when promotions on a particular brand cause consumers to purchase more of it. This dynamic is explained in the Blattberg trade promotion grid, developed by Professor Robert Blattberg of Northwestern University (see Exhibit 13.3).

Trade deals for products that have high holding costs are often successful because fewer future sales at the regular price are likely to be cannibalized. Products that have high holding costs tend to be items that are bulky relative to their cost or profit margin (such as toilet paper) or require refrigeration or other special storage (such as ice cream). Products that spoil quickly, such as potato chips or milk, may also fall into this category. In addition, products that are promotionally responsive (or, in economic terms, that have high price elasticities) are good prospects for trade deals, since a small decrease in price may result in a large increase in volume. This is especially true in situations when having more product in the home may cause individuals to consume the product at a higher rate (as may be the case with cookies, for example), or when switchers who might have purchased a competitor's brand in the future buy a product on deal and then stockpile it.

The trade promotion grid combines these two factors to predict the success of trade promotions for various types of products. For instance, a bulky product that is promotionally responsive, such as soft drinks, is a good prospect for a trade promotion. Because consumers will purchase more of the product if the price is lowered, retailers are likely to pass on the discount to consumers and advertise the special, producing a sharp increase in consumer sales. In addition, because retailers and consumers will find it expensive or impractical to store very much of the product, future sales at the full price will not be greatly cannibalized. The main problem with promoting this type of product is that manufacturers may find trade deals so successful that they overuse them, diluting the image of the brand and causing some consumers to purchase only on deal.

In situations where holding costs are high and promotional responsiveness is low, trade promotions are not likely to increase sales much for the manufacturer. Therefore, there may be little reason for manufacturers to promote them often. For instance, because large sizes of dry dog food are difficult to store and appeal to only a small percentage of the population, they tend to be promoted relatively infrequently.

When promotional responsiveness is high and holding costs are low, trade deals may produce extremely high incremental sales, as both consumers and retailers stock up. However, some of this volume increase is likely to be at the expense of future sales, due to the large amount of product being stockpiled by retailers or consumers or both. For example, retailers may pass an attractive deal on canned tuna fish on to consumers to get extra sales. However, since tuna is compact and easily stored, it also may be stockpiled in large quantities by retailers and consumers. In general, promotions on products in this category can be helpful provided that they are not used too frequently.

Brands that have low holding costs and low consumer responsiveness may see a sales spike with a trade promotion; however, nearly all the extra volume is likely to be borrowed from future sales, since retailers and consumers may stockpile the product. For instance, laxatives and other over-the-counter medications are compact and easy for retailers or consumers to store for long periods. In addition, promotional responsiveness for these products is likely to be limited, since only a finite number of consumers use any particular pharmaceutical, and since their usage of this kind of product is not likely to increase simply because they get a good deal on it. Brands that fall into this category generally are not good candidates for trade promotions, since immediate incremental volume is likely to be at the expense of long-term brand profitability.

Strategic Uses of Trade Deals

Trade deals are frequently cited as the most misused and overused form of sales promotion. However, when used appropriately, they can be useful in helping certain kinds of marketers to reach specific goals. (Much of this success, of course, depends on how much of the trade promotion is passed on to the consumer in the form of price reductions, advertising, trade coupons or displays. This section examines how consumers are likely to respond to deals when they are passed on by the retailer who receives them from manufacturers.)

Loyal Users

Trade promotions may encourage some current customers to remain loyal to a particular product rather than switching to a competitive brand. They may therefore be very effective when used as a countering move when competitors have begun (or are expected to begin) making active attempts to steal a brand's loyal customers (for instance, with heavy advertising, a new or reformulated product or a sampling program). However, often brand loyal consumers who buy a product that is on a retailer "special" would have purchased it anyway, either immediately or in the future.

Trade deals that are passed on to consumers may be very successful in getting loyal users to make additional purchases when the extra product may be easily consumed. For instance, an occasional user of the relatively high-priced General Foods International Coffees brand may purchase a can to have as a special treat if it is on discount.

Competitive Loyals

Trade deals are usually less successful than other promotions at getting competitive loyals to buy a particular brand, even when the discount is passed on to the consumer. Consumers who are consistently loyal to another brand probably won't be motivated to switch when presented with a simple price decrease, and possibly they won't even notice the promotion. However, trade deals, like other forms of sales promotion may help to convert competitive loyals when combined with other forms of promotion that catch these consumers' attention, such as advertising, public relations, or sweepstakes.

Switchers

People who switch for reasons of price or variety are often good targets for trade promotions. The increase in the number of switchers in the population has, in fact, probably been largely responsible for the increasing number of trade deals, as well as coupons, that have been offered by manufacturers in recent years.

Trade discounts can sometimes be effective in helping manufacturers gain or maintain distribution for a product. And although it is often considered negative that discounts can load the trade with product, increased inventories can help to ensure that the brand is never out of stock.

Price Buyers

Price buyers will often purchase a brand because it is on deal, provided that the special brings the price down to the level of that being charged for the least expensive competitive brands. Marketers who hope to generate volume from price buyers need to determine what price is currently being charged for other brands, and whether the retailer is likely to lower the price of the promoted brand to be competitive with the price leaders in the category.

Nonusers

Trade discounts are rarely effective at getting nonusers to try a brand in a category they don't use, since they don't give these people any reason to buy the product other than price.

Trade Promotions and Residual Value

Trade promotions are often seen as reducing the long-term value of brands. Consumers and retailers often use trade promotions as an opportunity to stock up on products, thereby reducing the number of purchases that they need to make in the future. In addition, too-frequent trade deals can teach consumers and retailers to purchase only when a brand is being promoted and to reevaluate the amount that brand appears to be "worth."

Whether this actually occurs, however, depends on the type of product being promoted and how frequently the discounts occur. Occasional promotions for appropriate products can often attract retailer and consumer attention to a particular product, persuading them to buy it, thereby increasing the likelihood that it will continue to be successful in the long run.

Index